$6

# THE
# ATLANTIC
# SHORE

*Illustrated by Edward and Marcia Norman*

# THE
# ATLANTIC
# SHORE

*Human and Natural History*
*from Long Island to Labrador*

BY

JOHN HAY and PETER FARB

PARNASSUS IMPRINTS
BOX 335, ORLEANS, MASS. 02653

*Other Books by John Hay*

The Great Beach
Nature's Year
The Run

*Other Books by Peter Farb*

Face of North America: The Natural History of a Continent
Living Earth
Land and Wildlife of North America
Ecology
The Insects
The Forest
The Story of Life

LIBRARY OF CONGRESS CATALOG CARD NUMBER: 66-13919

ISBN 0-940160-14-5

FOR Kristi Hay AND Oriole Farb

# CONTENTS

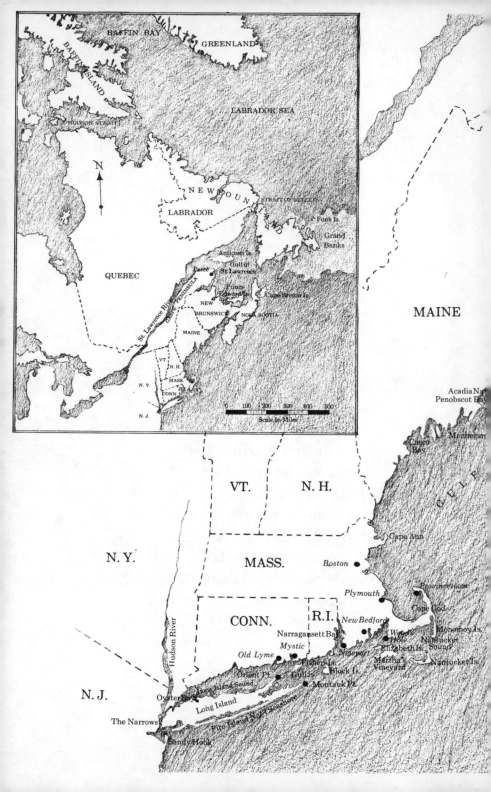

GASPÉ
PENINSULA

NEW BRUNSWICK

Prince Edward Is.

Cape Breton Is.

N O V A   S C O T I A

St. John

BAY OF FUNDY

Lubec

Grand
Manan Is.

Desert Is.

MAINE

A T L A N T I C   O C E A N

N

0        50        100
Scale In Miles

# SOUNDINGS

**1** ———————————————————————————————

BACK OF THE ATLANTIC COASTLINE, thousands of miles of it, progressing from giant icebergs floating in the sea, dark cliffs spotted or sheathed with snow, offshore islands, fir-studded ledges of granite, to low headlands, beaches, marshes, rivers, sand spits, and shoals, there was the enormous weight and power of an unknown continent—the power of nature, dark with unexampled dangers. The reality of it was enough to shrivel the spirit. Before we conquered and settled this land a vast wake of human casualties lay behind us. Our own contemporary power to reach out in space, to use nature for our own ends, to rule or misrule in a man-centered world, is in large measure the result of primal riches. We were made by what we overcame.

The grand outline is still there. Arctic air descends over vast reaches of territory and then recedes. The hurricanes strike on intermittent years out of their spawning grounds in the Caribbean. The Atlantic Ocean rocks gently or boils against the coast. A spruce tree on a Maine ledge, a codfish in offshore waters, a shad that still migrates up the Hudson in spite of polluted waters, the much-pursued lobster and the overdug clam, the herring gull, the cormorant, the hermit thrush, and the seaside sparrow, all give these original shores their character. They are still its true representatives, those we first met as strangers, new in a new land.

As nature, of course, the land was not new at all; it only seemed so to civilizations already old and "beautified," as Captain John Smith wrote in his *Description of New England* (1615), "by the long labor and diligence of industrious people and Art."

"This," the great promoter goes on to say, "is as God made it, when he created the worlde. Therefore I conclude if the heart and intralls of those Regions were sought: if their land were cultured, planted and manured by men of industrie, judgment and experience, what hope is there but it might equalize any of these famous Kingdoms?"

We are Pilgrim-oriented, and like to take the date of 1620 as our beginning, but as a settlement Plymouth had its temporary predecessors, and in the north at least, the landings of Columbus were predated by five hundred years. At L'Anse au Meadow in the northern tip of Newfoundland, on the grassy turf of a sandy, open, wind-blown shore, a Viking settlement has recently been uncovered that dates back to about 1000 A.D. Archaeologists have found outlines of houses, one of them a typical Viking hall, sixty by forty-five feet, with a hearth at its center. In some of the sites were stone fireplaces and "ember pits" where coals were kept alive during the night. A stone anvil was found, too, evidence that there had been a smithy for hammering iron found in nearby bogs.

These Norse settlers reached Newfoundland by way of Iceland and Greenland, traveling up Greenland's southwest coast into Davis Strait and then turning south down the coast of Labrador.

The Icelandic sagas which tell the story of the Norse discovery of "Vinland" seem to hint at further sailings along sandy shores to the south, most probably to Nova Scotia. They came in slim, open boats with single sails, navigating by sun and stars, driven off their course continually by wind and storms, losing their bearings in the fog, tossed for days and weeks on the open sea. In terms of direct distance, Iceland is some 150 nautical miles from Greenland, and Baffin Island another 200 miles across Davis Strait from Greenland, with a longer stretch down the coast to Newfoundland; and it is remarkable, a tribute to their great fortitude and skill, that they made the trip not once but several times.

The sagas tell of northern shores and islands washed by strong ocean currents, of a multitude of eider ducks, of whales, of salmon in inland rivers and lakes, of woods teeming with animals, and creeks full of fish; and they speak of the violent and superstitious feelings the Norse explorers brought with them, of omens and premonitions. Their encounters with the Indians or Eskimos, whom they called "Skraellings," a name denoting worthlessness, were savage—often murderous in the extreme, though there was some trading in cloth and furs—and were probably the chief reason why they abandoned their settlement and went back to Iceland for good.

After these stark beginnings, Newfoundland and the northeast coast were not visited again for centuries, so far as we know, although Basque whalers were off Newfoundland at an early date, probably by the end of the fourteenth century. Then European fishermen began to extend their fishing grounds from the North Sea, Ireland, and Iceland, until they were crossing the waters to the Grand Banks of Newfoundland with increasing frequency as the great sixteenth-century period of exploration came on.

The anonymous fishermen, thousands of individuals involved in a common, dangerous trade, men from the edge, the reaches of their civilization, were the next, then, after the Viking sea warriors to open the way to North America and to keep in contact with it. Their incentive was not so much the desire to explore the mysteries of a new land as to provide Catholic Europe with its staple diet of fish. Competition, not curiosity, was what sent them on. Much has been made, and justifiably, of the great explorers who found and won these continental shores, but the fishermen had taken the first needed steps. Few of their names have come down to us, and there are only hints of various obscure quarrels and misadventures that happened to them over the centuries. Their ships were small. They left very little in the way of maps or detailed descriptions. On the other hand, these ships not only brought back holds laden with fish but talk that filtered through the taverns of European ports, and helped spur on other ships to sail westward and explore the new world. (It may be added that they were also in part responsible for the blended nationalities of which we still find evidence in Newfoundland and New England.)

Line trawling employed a thousand vessels a year as early as 1550 off the Grand Banks, and though a number of different kinds of fish had been noted there at an early date, the staple catch was the cod, or what the Indians called "baccalaos." The cod were large and they were abundant, so much so that fishermen took what they wanted and threw the rest overboard. These men— whether Breton, Basque, Portuguese, or English—were bent on fishing the banks between early spring and July, loading as much fish into their holds as possible and returning to Europe without delay. This practice was known as "wet" or "green" fishing. Dousing the cod with large amounts of salt was sufficient to prevent decay until they could be cured in home ports.

However, as fishermen continued to set foot on the new shores and to make temporary claims on harbors, coves, and beaches, they also undertook a different method of curing, which was not startling but was to have major consequences. In fact it helped open the new continent to exploration. The seasonal stays of these fishermen on the mainland were long enough now so that they could prepare the fish before stowing them on board. The flesh of the cod is gelatinous without being fatty, and so could easily be cured with a light salting and a slow drying in the sun. Once back in Europe the flesh could be restored to something like its original taste and texture merely by restoring the water.

This "dry" curing, a process taking several months, brought the fishermen from offshore banks to temporary settlements along the beaches or rocky shores. This meant anchorages, watering places, lumber for building houses and sheds, which in turn brought more exploration and closer contact with the natives. These early meetings with the Indians foreshadowed the white man's relationship with them for the next four centuries. The fishermen began to act as the settlers would at a later date: They logged the scant timber of Newfoundland, usurped ancient hunting and fishing grounds, took over camping sites and water supplies. The Indians—they are thought to have been Canadian Iroquois—must have watched uncomprehendingly as the Europeans wasted their land; but they did not watch for long. They were extinct all along the shores of mainland Canada by about 1600, though the last survivor of the Beothuk, natives of Newfoundland, died there in 1829. As for the land, one early observer found that the woods along the shore of Newfoundland were "so spoyled by the fishermen that it is a great pity to behold them, and without redresse undoubtedly it will be ruine of this good land."

The fishermen's temporary settlements and explorations on the mainland, their contacts with the Indians, also resulted in opening up another great resource, the fur trade. As early as 1503, Frenchmen traveling into the Gulf of St. Lawrence had begun to use beach stations for trading in furs with the Indians. The skins of marten, beaver, elk, and deer were all in demand in Europe, especially the dark fur of the marten, which was reserved for royal courts. To find beaver, whose downy pelts were shorn to make the hats then in fashion, explorers first captured the animals near the shore, but then began to track them farther inland, up the water courses where they had their homes. Over the next two centuries this quest led the Europeans farther and farther into the American continent, passing the Continental Divide as the beaver frontier receded westward.

Who, these days, could conceive that a beaver trade once flourished on the shores of Connecticut? Still, the Dutch explorer Adriaen mentioned it in 1614 as located in the general area of New Haven, although he does not give the local Indians much credit for energy in its pursuit. "The natives who dwell here are called Quinipeys. They take many beavers, but it is necessary for them to get into the habit of trade, otherwise they are too indolent to hunt the beaver." Indolence was not the cause so much as limited technology. The stone tools of an Indian could hardly compete with a steel ax from Europe, which could be used to break into a beaver lodge with comparative ease and to kill the animals before they escaped under water.

So there was a direct and practical link between the early fishermen and the development of fur trading and exploration, even though we hear only about the explorers; and in fact it was the fishermen's daring and enterprise that made conquest and settlement a reality. Sixteenth-century exploration begins with the landfall of John Cabot, possibly at Cape Breton, Nova Scotia, in 1497, and ends with the Pilgrims in 1620, by which time the entire length of the northern coast had not only been traveled by European ships, but had also been mapped, which is not to say that it was known in depth. Reading the early accounts, one feels that the Europeans had to spar for a long time with the reality of the continent, in spite of all the rich catalogues it inspired them to compile.

At first glance, it might seem amazing to us that in the early decades of this burst of exploration on the part of four great

European nations, ships patroling the coast could still lack real knowledge of the three great water-entries into the heart of the continent: the Hudson River, the St. Lawrence, and Hudson Bay. But these coasts, with their shallows and shrouds of mist and ice, were a formidable challenge for a vessel to follow, much less to chart. Two great currents, the Labrador and the Gulf Stream, upset the sailor's reckoning. The fogs they caused were frequent, and icebergs were a hazard even during the summer. The profusion of islands along the shore from Maine northward led most of the early explorers to visualize the new continent as little more than an archipelago of islands large and small. The islands were fewer as the explorers worked southward down the coast, but there sand dunes, spits, and barrier islands masked the entrances to inland rivers. Because their ships were not rigged to sail with any ease into the wind, they did not always have the time to investigate the shoreline with any thoroughness, but had to take advantage of any favorable wind when it came.

The great enterprise continued, with both fishermen and explorers following the shorelines along the coast; and the fringes of this new world—hot and fever-ridden at one end and an icy desolation at the other, but with magnificent forests in between, and uncounted natural riches everywhere—began to be named and recognized. They probed and sounded:

So we steered away south south-east all night and had ground until the middle of the third watch. Then we had fortie-five fathoms, white sand and little stones. So all our soundings are twentie, twentie, twentie-two, twentie-seven, thirtie-two, fortie-three, fortie-five—then no ground in seventie fathoms.

In this ship's record you can hear Henry Hudson's mate Robert Juet sounding along the coast, a man who was to take part in the mutiny that left Hudson a frozen corpse in Hudson Bay, his great discovery.

The actual human experience of meeting these mighty shores and their approaches for the first time, the deep intrinsic history, is unbridgeable. We can sense dimly the original wildness of the land, for here and there patches of it still remain, but time and human conquest have cut us off. Still, some of the early accounts do manage to convey the awe and mystery felt by the men in those approaching ships. Martin Frobisher sailed westward from the Orkney Islands off northern Scotland to search for "the passage to China," and on the way he encountered driftwood, carried eastward by the Gulf Stream: "We met floting in the sea, great Firre trees, which as we judged, were with the furie of great floods rooted up, and so driven into the sea. It seemeth, that these trees are driven from some part of the New found land, with the current that setteth from the West to the East." (Note the divided spelling of Newfoundland, which today is accented on the last syllable in that province and in Nova Scotia.)

As Frobisher and his men sailed on, like others before and after them, they came through storms: "Boisterous Boreal blast mixed with snow and haile, in the months of June and July." The ship was hemmed in by thick fogs through which sea birds suddenly appeared as a hopeful sign of land, and then there were great islands of ice which "fell one part from another, making a noyse as if a great cliffe had fallen into the sea." In the thick fogs off Baffin Land, Labrador, and Newfoundland, these Elizabethans had no way of keeping track of each other except by occasional shots or by sounding their drums and trumpets. After encountering such a "hidious mist" that a nearby ship was lost to sight, Frobisher's chronicler recorded: "We stroke our drums, and sounded our trumpets, to the ende we might keepe together: and so continued all that day and night till the next day that the mist brake up."

The fishermen did not lead the way to exploration nor to permanent settlement without practical assistance. Successful expeditions depended on good organization and the backing of merchants at home. The early exploration by Giovanni Caboto, formerly of Genoa and Venice, whose name was later anglicized to John Cabot, appealed for just such practical support from the merchants of the English port of Bristol, and he succeeded in getting it. He sailed westward in May, 1497, to explore New-foundland and Nova Scotia, and was back home in less than three months. After this first brief reconnaissance of the North Atlantic shore, the voyages by John and his son Sebastian were to continue until 1509.

The Cabots brought back information calculated to whet mer-cantile appetites. Sebastian did concede that Labrador had "soil barren in some places," but he was also able to talk of "stags far greater than ours" (meaning, presumably, the caribou), and he reported fishes, some as great as seals, "soles above a yard in length," and, of course, the abundant baccalaos, which seem to have been commented on by every explorer approaching New-foundland. The fish were so abundant, the Cabots reported, that they could be "caught not merely with nets but with baskets."

In spite of the clear and tangible riches that the explorers found before their eyes, the land still lay hidden behind the breakers, and so long as it remained unknown it was a realm of myth. Because the explorers thought they were within reach of the spice lands of Asia, a polar bear sighted by John Cabot was taken for one of the beasts of Cathay. As time went on, they gave up the idea that they were searching for the shortest route to the fabulous East and recognized the new continent in its own right.

Perhaps the full sweep of the North Atlantic shore in all its reality was first seen by Giovanni di Verrazano, who was sent out in 1523 by the king of France, and who made his first landfall in the vicinity of Cape Fear, North Carolina. After some inconclu-sive tacking off the Carolinas he turned north. Hugging the coast, he came to "a very agreeable situation located within two small prominent hills, in the midst of which flowed to the sea a very great river, which was deep within its mouth." He had stumbled upon the Hudson River and New York Harbor. Sailing to the east he encountered an island "full of hills covered with trees," which is thought to have been Block Island, lying between the eastern tip of Long Island and the Rhode Island shore. Verrazano seems to have exaggerated the abundance of the trees, for explorations not long afterwards described them as "brush-wood"; but even those thickets have long since been cut over, and all attempts at growing trees there were frustrated by the livestock that trampled and ate the seedlings.

Due north of Block Island, Verrazano came to "a very beautiful port"–Narragansett Bay–where he remained for two weeks, delighting in the surrounding land's "charming hills with many brooks, which from the height to the sea discharged clean waters." These hills are now fully exploited by human commerce and housing, and the few brooks that still have clear water trickle into a polluted bay. Verrazano explored the interior of Rhode Island to a distance of somewhat less than twenty miles. He gives us the earliest picture we have of the lands behind the beaches and rocks of the northeast coast where he found well-tended agricultural fields "open and devoid of every impediment of trees . . . any seed in them would produce the best crops." The Narragansett Indians were probably the most proficient farmers of the northeast coast, but explorers also found such plots elsewhere along many other parts of the shore. Behind them there were burned-over forest glades and woods culled for timber by the Indians.

Verrazano observed that in this bay "any numerous fleet, without fear of tempest or other impediment of fortune, could rest securely," thus anticipating the port of Providence and the U.S. Naval Training Station at Newport. He sailed north along the coast of New England, passing Cape Cod, which, oddly enough, he took to be a shoal, and eventually reached the mouth of the Kennebec River. Unfortunately he left no detailed description of the shore but he did describe what is now Maine as "a huge land full of very thick forests, the trees of which were pine, cypresses and such as grow in cold regions." As he progressed farther north toward the fishing grounds, he learned that the aborigines had already encountered southward-straying fishermen. The inhabitants of Maine, which Verrazano called "the land of bad people," behaved in sharp contrast to the peaceful Narragansetts. The Maine Indians had already learned to drive a shrewd bargain with Europeans; they would not permit Verrazano to visit their villages, and they attacked one of his armed parties on shore. Happy to leave, he sailed up the coast to Nova Scotia, passing Maine's multitudinous islands, and greatly admiring them. Then he skirted the Bay of Fundy and turned back toward France.

Verrazano's accomplishment was tremendous. He filled in the gap between the probings of the Spanish along the south Atlantic shore and the explorations of the "New Founde Land" to the north. He proved that here was a true continent, not just an archipelago or isthmus of Asia. Now the charting could begin in earnest. The first of the segments to be filled in, namely the Gulf of St. Lawrence, bounded by Newfoundland, Quebec, New Brunswick, and Nova Scotia, known simply as the "Great Bay" during the early days of exploration, was thoroughly explored in the name of France by Jacques Cartier's three voyages between 1534 and 1543. Like the other explorers, he was impressed by the great fisheries and the sea-bird colonies but disappointed by Labrador, calling it "the land God gave to Cain." However, once he had circumnavigated the gulf, he found much to be enthusiastic about. He admired the majesty of the cliffs at Quebec's Gaspé Peninsula and saw the gannets, guillemots, murres, and gulls that gathered there in such abundance. He also praised Prince Edward Island: "Two acres of it are worth more than the whole of Newfoundland." He did not overlook the possibility of exploiting the white whales (belugas) and the herds of walruses and seals for oil, hides, bones, and ivory. Seals are still seen in the gulf, but the whales and walruses have long since disappeared from its waters. The huge walruses must have added to the already impressive character of the landscape, described by Cartier as composed of "stones and horrible rocks." They were "great beasts like large oxen, which have two tusks in their jaw like elephants' tusks." The Atlantic walrus once ranged as far south as Massachusetts, although its most southerly breeding colony was located at Sable Island, Nova Scotia. This colony was butchered to extinction little more than a hundred years after Cartier explored the Gulf of St. Lawrence. Today the walrus is a rare sight south of Labrador.

Cartier made the important discovery that the St. Lawrence "grew narrower as one approached Canada, and also that farther up, the water became fresh." Cartier had seen how the gulf narrowed from about three hundred miles on its eastern side to a mere twenty miles near Anticosti Island on the west, and he assumed correctly that the St. Lawrence's torrent of fresh water poured out of the interior of the continent. On subsequent voyages, he was to travel a thousand miles up the river, pausing at the Indian village that would later become Montreal, only to find that he had not yet reached the western side of the continent.

Of all Cartier's descriptions of landscapes, forests, and wildlife, none gives us so great a sense of loss as his picture of the rocky islands swarming with so many sea birds "that all the ships of France might load a cargo of them without once perceiving that any had been removed." Until the arrival of the European fishing fleets these birds were relatively secure from human enemies on their high and jagged islands, but sailors welcomed a change from their diet of salt meat and fish, and so the attack upon the bird islands began in earnest. "These islands were as completely covered with birds," Cartier observed, "as a field is covered with grass." Even three hundred years later, after countless thousands of

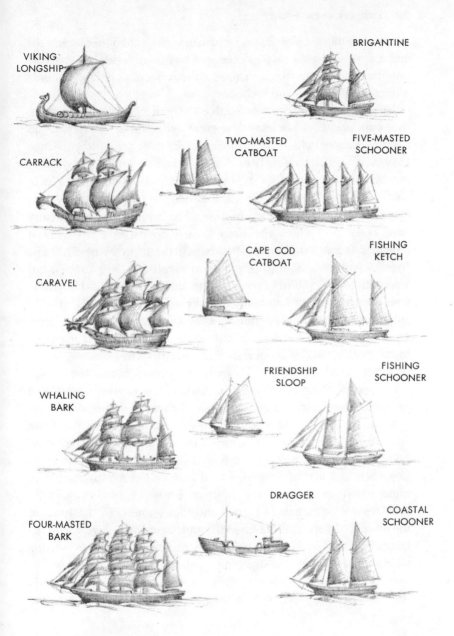

VIKING LONGSHIP

BRIGANTINE

CARRACK

TWO-MASTED CATBOAT

FIVE-MASTED SCHOONER

CARAVEL

CAPE COD CATBOAT

FISHING KETCH

WHALING BARK

FRIENDSHIP SLOOP

FISHING SCHOONER

FOUR-MASTED BARK

DRAGGER

COASTAL SCHOONER

gannets, puffins, eider ducks, and other birds had been clubbed and trampled to death by successive waves of meat hunters, the population of these islands, though it may seem very large, is only a fraction of what it used to be.

One species, however, was unable to fly or clamber to safety up sheer, rocky walls. The flightless great auk, called a "penguin" in early narratives, which once ranged at least as far south as Cape Cod, now went into a swift decline. Hakluyt described the manner in which it was started on its way to extinction: "We had sight of an Iland named Penguin, of a foule there breeding in abundance, almost incredible, which cannot flie, their wings not able to carry their body . . . which the French men use to take up without difficulty from that Iland and to barrell them up with salt." The Indians had been able to reach these islands in their canoes, but after killing a few birds they went on their way again. The Europeans, on the other hand, filled casks with the carcasses of auks and took them on their long sea voyages as a supply of food. From that time the great auk had no future, although it managed to stave off extinction for some three centuries after Cartier.

South of the Gulf of St. Lawrence and Nova Scotia the explorers sounded along the shores, in harbors, bays, rivers, and tidal grounds. They made observations about them and also about hills and islands, rocks and minerals, fir trees and hardwoods, fishes and birds. They noted in detail how Indians constructed their houses and canoes, how they sowed their crops of beans and corn, how they looked and dressed, fished and fought. With respect to these native Americans, the trials in brutality and restraint on both sides were endless. This nip and tuck game with the Indians, the mutual feasts and trading, the outbursts of savagery and retaliation, was the kind of game the explorers were also playing with an awesome and savage land.

If the northeast coast was often a cold and dangerous place in the sixteenth and seventeenth centuries, it was also rich in a natural life that had hardly been interfered with for time untold, an abundance that was constantly referred to by the explorers themselves as "unbelievable." The seas were teeming with life, the trees were gigantic, the birds innumerable, the spring and summer shores were fragrant and inviting. In the explorers' accounts, the details of the natural history are uncertain, but not its extent and variety.

Among many motives—fish, furs, or a meeting with oriental potentates—that may have impelled the explorers to fill in blank spaces on the map of the New England shore, none is more curious than Captain Bartholomew Gosnold's search for sassafras root. The same fickle fashion that could send ships across the seas for pelts to make hats could also conjure up a demand for this medicinal wonder plant, which grew only in America. When soaked in water, its roots were supposed to discourage bedbugs, heal broken bones, halt fever and falling hair, increase manly vigor and act as a general tonic. As a cure for "the French poxe," or syphilis, it became so widely known that no European gentleman would be seen drinking sassafras tea in public, lest he be thought infected and taking the cure. Whole shiploads of sassafras were transported to Europe, and as the price soared in European markets, Gosnold became only one of many English, French, and Spanish explorers to seek it out on the North American coast.

In 1602, Gosnold made his landfall along "a white sandy and very bold shore," where he found "better fishing, and in as great plentie, as in Newfoundland." Like earlier fishermen, his sailors caught such an abundance of cod that they were soon throwing the excess overboard. From then on, the place of his landing was known as Cape Cod, although it had previously been a conspicuous landmark for sailors who knew it under other names.

Gosnold's description of Cape Cod, written by a member of his crew, sounds like a piece of promotion literature: "But not to cloy you with particular rehearsall of such things as God and nature hath bestowed on these places, in comparison whereof, the most fertile part of New England is of itself but barren. . . ." Exploring the shore, the men found meadows and clear lakes and sweet soil. There were high-timbered oaks, cedar, beech, elm, holly, and walnut, and also sassafras. They were particularly impressed by the berries they found in great profusion—strawberries, gooseberries, raspberries and "whortleberries" (which may have been cranberries).

Rounding Cape Cod and heading southwest, Gosnold reached the island he named Martha's Vineyard because of grapevines so abundant that they "runne upon every tree," and "they could not goe for treading upon them." But these plants were only the beginning of the catalogue of plenty. Trading with Indians, the men obtained the skins of beaver, marten, wildcat, otter, black fox, rabbit, seal, and deer. Other lists are of birds, such as cranes, bitterns, geese, mallards, and teal, along with other species which are either not designated specifically or else given such fanciful names that we cannot guess what they may have been. Though his observations were incomplete, Gosnold's quest for sassafras resulted in the first faunal and floral inventory of the northeastern coast. The richness of his catalogue and of those that followed stand in sharp contrast to the sparse descriptions given by the Cabots a century before.

The shape of the northeast coast was now becoming discernible. Another segment between the Bay of Fundy and Massachusetts Bay was filled in by Samuel de Champlain, who in 1604 cruised south down the coast of Maine to where the notched, granite mountain blocks of a great island faced the sea. The pink-granite heights of Mount Desert Island are no less grand today than they were then, but the enormous pines seen by Champlain—some of which lingered into the early nineteenth century only as huge rotting stumps—are now gone, and even the spruce woods have been sadly depleted by the ax and recent disastrous fires.

Cruising back and forth along the Maine coast, Champlain explored what he called the "delightful" region of Penobscot Bay and penetrated inland as far as the falls at Bangor. In the area of the Saco River, Champlain's Frenchmen found the forests supporting a tangle of grapevines which they thought would yield "a very good" wine. Running south to Boston Harbor, Champlain was impressed by the extent of the agricultural lands near the shore and by the stands of oak, red cedar, and hickory. The Indians had already cleared much of the coastal forest in this area, and in only a few decades the Europeans would continue the job so thoroughly that Boston ended up timber-poor.

Champlain put in at Plymouth, where he found an extensive population of Indians carrying on their fishing and agriculture. The fame of Plymouth dates to the settlement of the Pilgrims there in 1620, but its harbor had been well known for nearly two decades before that—in 1604 Martin Pring described it as "an excellent Haven at the entrance whereof we found twentie fathoms water and rode at our ease in seven fathoms being Land-locked, the Haven winding in compass like the shell of a Snaile. . . ." It was named in 1614 by Captain John Smith in honor of the English port in Devonshire. The Plymouth area was so heavily farmed that the Indians produced an annual surplus of corn, which they stored in deep trenches in the sand. It was the discovery of one of these stores of "Indian" corn with its kernels "of diverce colors," that helped the hungry Pilgrims survive their first winter in the New World. Before returning to Canada, Champlain cruised the waters of Cape Cod and recorded that this jutting peninsula had the "form of a sickell."

Champlain also found the air filled with passenger pigeons "in infinite numbers." Now that these birds are extinct, after making a final stand around the Great Lakes at the end of the last century, it is hard to visualize their former abundance, even along the northeastern shores. At the time of Audubon their numbers in the

United States probably equaled those of all other breeding land birds combined.

The lists of plants and animals made by the explorers sometimes read as if they had been drawn hastily, or were imitative of a previous list, but a careful observer like Champlain described things in terms of color, shape, action, and size so that even now his descriptions come alive. A horseshoe crab he saw on Cape Cod was "a fish with a shell on its back like a tortoise, yet different, there being in the middle a row of little prickles, of the color of a dead leaf, like the rest of the fish." (Champlain may be excused for classifying the horseshoe crab as a fish, since it perplexed zoologists until the latter part of the nineteenth century, when they finally concluded that it was not a crab at all, but the sole survivor of a very ancient group of sea animals related to the spiders and scorpions.) His description continued:

The length of the tail varies according to their size. With the end of it these people [the Indians] pointed their arrows, and it contains also a row of prickles like the large shell in which are their eyes. There are eight small feet like those of the crab, and two behind longer and flatter, which they use in swimming. There are also in front two other very small ones with which they eat. Under the small shell there are membranes which swell up, and beat like the throat of a frog, and rest upon each other like the folds of a waistcoat. The largest specimen of this fish that I saw was a foot broad and a foot and a half long.

All in all, a very respectable description for an age in which sea monsters were still a dreaded reality.

Although Captain Martin Pring was cruising the Maine and Massachusetts coasts at about the same time as Champlain, he adds little new information to the descriptions of land and wildlife. Rather, he confirms what other explorers had observed along a shore that was becoming less and less mysterious. The fogs still descended on the coast, and the hazards of the sea were as real as ever; yet there must have been a growing confidence in the explorations and their successful outcome. Captain Pring makes the usual comment on the abundance of cod, and like previous explorers he is impressed by the Indians' crops and by the "strawberries very faire and bigge, Gooseberries, Raspices, Hurts [probably huckleberries] and other wild fruits." He had found sassafras, which he, too, says is "of sovereign virtue for the French poxe." He also made a good listing of the trees: "Vines, Cedars, Oakes, Ashes, Beeches, Birch trees, Cherrie trees bearing fruit whereof we did eat, Hasel, Witch-Hasels . . . Walnut trees, Maples, holy. . . . There were likewise a white kind of Plums which were grown to their perfect ripenesse. With divers other sorts of trees to us unknown." Unlike other explorers, he is not solely concerned with the fur-bearing mammals, but speaks of various members of the deer family, porcupines, "Beares, Wolves, Foxes, Lusernes, and (some say) Tygres." The "Lusernes" were either Canada lynx or bobcats and the "Tygres" probably were mountain lions. In primeval America mountain lions were extremely abundant in the northeast, but they are now limited to the western part of the continent and the Gulf Coast, with an isolated population in Florida, though they are occasionally rumored to have been sighted in the woodland areas of northern New England.

These subdued, matter-of-fact, and largely accurate accounts of the natural history of the new shore were overshadowed by the copious writings of that formidable pamphleteer Captain John Smith, hero of battles against the Turks, colonist of Virginia, sometime whaler and cartographer. Still not satisfied after this extraordinary career, Smith went on to set the stage for colonizing the northeast by hiring himself out in the year 1614 to London merchants as a reporter on the New World.

He found everything there abundant and ready for the taking. He even extolled the New England climate, about which most of the inhabitants have been complaining ever since the Pilgrims landed. He found the timber tall and the soil good, and was still more enthusiastic about the fisheries, the teeming shallows, the shores thick with lobsters, oysters, and clams. He reported that there was scarcely

any Baye, shallow shore, or Cove of sand, where you may not take many Clampes, or Lobsters, or both at your pleasure; and in many places lode your boate if you please . . . nor Isles where you find not fruits, birds, crabs, and muskles, or all of them for the taking, at a lowe water. And in the harbors we frequented, a little boy might take of Cunners and Pinnacks and such delicate fish, at the ship's sterne, more than sixe or tenne can eate in a daie; but with a casting net, thousand when wee pleased.

Though Captain Smith declared that if anyone failed to reap rewards in this bounteous country, "worthie is that Person to starve," the fact is that only four years later, the abundance notwithstanding, the Pilgrims almost did starve. They were saved only by finding Indian fields already cleared for agriculture, and by their discovery of surplus stores of corn. It was also their good fortune to meet the Indian Squanto, who taught them how to probe in the mud for eels, and how to harvest shellfish and, in the spring, the alewives running inland to spawn.

The history of exploration had advanced from the tentative probings by John Cabot to that first fearful settlement of the Pilgrims, clinging to the coast and the reassuring presence of the sea, at the edge of "a hideous wilderness, full of wild beasts and wild men." A great change had taken place. The European world now recognized that there was no shortcut to Cathay and was excited at coming to grips with the realities of this New World, spurred on, in greed and rivalry, to bridge the gap across the Atlantic seas.

The conquest then started was not only of the Indians but of all that was in the way to be taken—the high standing trees, the wild turkey, the otter, the wolf, the great auk, the sweet prodigality of these spring shores; and it is not over yet, although we may now be close to realizing that what is left will only be kept if we admit our need of it.

# THE STRUCTURE OF THE LAND

## 2

For most of us, landfalls are more apt to be made by dropping down out of the air than by plowing through the waves, and we may pass over the Atlantic almost without realizing it. In a very real and physical sense, what Francis Parkman called "the shaggy continent from Florida to the Pole, outstretched in savage slumber along the sea," the primal shore met by the fishermen, explorers, and settlers, is a thing of the past. A land which was once relatively uninhabited and rich in living things almost without parallel has become overlaid by a veneer of civilization. The bare sea lies along a man-scarred earth, with endless grids of buildings and streets, and even a man-made atmosphere, showing in palls of smoke and hazy air. Along many parts of the shore, trees seem to exist on human sufferance, shellfish are polluted or missing altogether, the flotsam of storm-hurled living things upon the beach now includes rubber tires, tar, and beer cans.

Human civilization has a tendency to insulate itself from the weather and to rearrange the environment to suit its purposes. This is a relatively new factor in the life of earth, in any event a factor which has gained vastly in influence during the last few thousand years, so that in considering the natural landscape of the Atlantic shore we cannot avoid taking it into account—but neither should we exaggerate it. The sea still swings on its old location, and we are affected in many subtle ways by the ebb and flow of the tides, by the seasons, and by night and day, just as we are often at the mercy of fogs on the highway and snow-laden winds howling through the shoreline trees. Ice in winter is packed by winds into Cape Cod Bay so that it looks like a white arctic sea. Cold driving winds come to the shore as a result of storm systems from the north and west. A huge spinning hurricane, spawned in the Caribbean, roars up the coastline and blows out to sea off Nova Scotia. The surfaces of the gray-green Atlantic rock and foam under winter winds, or loll and glitter in the warmth of summertime. The traveler along the shore, or one who makes it his home, may come to the discovery that this coast is more than "progress" can add to or detract from, that it is more than a scene or an object of use.

The boundaries of wind and weather and all the varying tenacities of natural life go beyond the shore; they belong to the wide world. In that sense, the coast is not easily divided into segments or categories. It is only a part, though a great one, of a shore that sweeps down to tropic waters and up to the gradually deepening Arctic. In fact, following the northward arc as the early sailors did, a European can land-hop to America by way of Iceland, Greenland, and Labrador. For all the hundreds of miles of open water in between, one continent is a geographical extension of the other, and for migrant marine animals and even some species of land life that are the same in Newfoundland and in England, it is all one shore.

Yet the North American coast is definite enough, even in its various subdivisions. For example, Cape Hatteras, North Carolina, amounts to a boundary, if a somewhat loose one, between warm and cold waters, a contrast of temperatures that affects the distribution of marine animals and other life along the shore. Cape Cod as a boundary has a similar claim. Cape Cod Bay, on the northern side, is an extension of the Gulf of Maine, and its waters are several degrees cooler than those of Nantucket Sound on the south. There are also differences in onshore climate, which is not the same, for example, in Connecticut as it is in Massachusetts.

What is referred to as the North Atlantic coast in this book comprises the coastal fringe between Labrador and the Hudson River, ending at Staten Island and Long Island, New York. This definition has been guided by the physical nature of the land itself, its recent history, and its present appearance. Northward from New York City the flexible crust of the earth was bent under the weight of ice sheets a mile thick, and, after the glacier melted, the entire coast was drowned. Much of it remains so today, and it will be drowned for the unknown years required for the earth, relieved of its burden, to spring back. The ice sheet left most of the coast stony, in contrast to southern shores with their great sandy plains sweeping down to the sea, and it also changed the distribution of plant and animal communities.

The northeast coast never has had a static relationship with the sea. The present configuration of the shoreline came about in relatively recent time, a matter of several thousand years. A great deal that was above the sea in pre-glacial times is now beneath it. On the other hand, some of the headlands now standing above salt water were once submerged by it, in a remote geologic era.

The coast's irregularity is eloquent with respect to change. In a sense, this is not one coast but many. A thousand feet or a thousand inches, although they may seem monotonous or uniform to the casual glance, prove on closer inspection to comprise many different physical environments, with varying juxtapositions of sand, rock, mud, or gravel, each with its own character, outline, and distinctive forms of life. The coastline is really no line at all, but rather many mergings from point to point in an indefinite series. Each bay, cove, marsh, or inlet provides a particular indentation. Each yard, in a major or minor way, reveals the shoreline's contact with the sea, the points of assault by storm waves, regions of tidal entry, the sea's effect in accumulating material or taking it away.

When we think of the coast, we have to imagine its underwater extensions sloping away beyond the shore as well as the emerged land. These submerged areas are part of the continental shelf, a gently sloping terrace starting at the shoreline and extending out into deep water, where, at depths of fifty to seventy fathoms, the continental slope begins. The shelf varies greatly in width, from a few miles off Miami to three hundred miles in the vicinity of Newfoundland. Its depths are consistent over broad reaches beyond the coastline but in others they are irregular. The water is about three hundred feet deep over some parts of the Grand Banks, but comparatively shallow in others. The shelf is shallowest over Georges Bank, east of Cape Cod, where the water in some places is no deeper than twenty feet.

As evidence that the continental shelf was once dry land, peat has been brought up from the Georges Bank area and carbon-dated by radioactivity at 11,000 years. A mastodon's tooth has also been found. If that ancient animal had died there and the tooth had not simply been transported by the glacier, it must have lived at a time when the sea level was much lower than it is today.

The exposed part of the coast, from irregular rocky headlands to curving sandy beaches, is influenced from day to day by the rhythmic retreats and advances of the sea, just as it has been over vast stretches of geologic time. Erosion and deposition, building up and taking away, are the processes that continually shape the shore. What the sea removes from one place, it returns to another. Twice daily the tides scour the bottom beyond the low-tide line, repositioning its stones, mud, and sand, to however slight a de-gree. Along sandy shores this material may be transported parallel to the land by offshore currents. Along rocky shores it may be ground and tumbled by the surf. Storm waves have the greatest impact on the shore, having a force sometimes of as much as twenty tons per square yard. These waves are augmented in their destructive power by the stones they carry forward and hurl against a cliff or headland. They can also compress air between the cracks and crevices of rocks so as to break them farther apart by the great pressure that results. Eventually storm waves and the lesser action of the surf may so undercut a cliff that sections of it come crashing down. Then the waves continue their process of destruction, breaking down the debris into smaller rocks and stones that serve as projectiles to be hurled against the cliffs again.

Different kinds of rock vary in their hardness, and some of the hardest persist for a long time at the base of the cliff from which they were cut. But, in the end, erosion reduces even these rocks to pebbles which will be ground still further into finer particles of sand and mud. Sand is easily transported by offshore currents to form and reform beaches in the bays and sheltered areas along the coast, often in a complicated give and take relationship with underwater shoals. Even along rock shores enough erosion will occur to build up small and intermittent beaches, some of them composed almost entirely of pebbles and stones.

Glacial ice, changing climates, the sea, have all had their long fetches and withdrawals in consonance with continental rise and fall over so long a time that even the accumulated knowledge of geology cannot quite encompass it. Rocks hard or soft, whether they are in Nova Scotia, Maine, or Connecticut have equally complex histories in the sequence of earth's events. What is displayed before the eye sometimes stands up like some appalling monument to an age beyond ages, as compared with the fluid present. Alongside one rocky cove in southern Newfoundland there is a high, dark cliff of sandstone whose surfaces are marked with ripples, clearly visible even though these marks were left by the sea some six hundred million years ago. It is easier to comprehend the results of our more "recent" glacial age—the stones dropped by the moving glaciers across a Connecticut field; the "glacial erratic," a huge boulder now perched on top of Cadillac Mountain at Mount Desert Island after having been swept there by ice from far inland; the notches cut in that island's mountain block; the ridge where the glacier ended down the center of Cape Cod.

Still, the past, no matter how distant, is amalgamated with the present in the earth's structure, there to be read, so that the steadiness of its processes are as much to be wondered at as its age. Shifts in the earth's crust have tilted up sea beds of great antiquity even as others were being laid down. In parts of Cape Breton, Nova Scotia, there are low inland cliffs of gypsum, soft and white, left behind by the evaporation of an ancient sea from a time when the climate was hot and semi-arid, and the marine life subtropical. In coves along the shore in that same region, broken-off chunks of gypsum cliffs that are continually splashed by sea water have become soapy smooth; and as the sea erodes cliffs of shale it reveals fossil ferns and reptiles. There are also high cliffs composed of sea sediment and tiny fossil shells; and enormous chunks of red sandstone divide and come crashing down as the sea erodes the land, uncovering new records of ancient life. There are rocks buckled and contorted under pressure that look like so much living tissue caught in a vise. Nearby remnants of great swamps show their presence by veins of coal, and iron-hard basaltic rock records a lava flow that covered the northern part of Nova Scotia during an ancient period of volcanic activity.

Ages exist side by side, land upheaved and in strange juxtapositions. Millions of years of stress and strain are evident in newly-formed rock lying on top of still more ancient rock, a record of sudden violence as well as of long and gradual adjustment. The granite we see in Maine, or along the southern coast of Nova Scotia, once welled up out of the earth as enormous molten masses invading a cover of still older rock. The gray ledges of schist at Pemaquid Point in Maine were formed by pressure miles under the surface of the earth. Today they are exposed to salt spray, storm waves, sun, and wind, and long broken sections of the rock lie along the surface like the ruined columns of a Greek temple.

The shore that has changed so greatly in character over the millennia is always changing, however imperceptibly, from day to day and even from hour to hour. On a hard rock coast, to be sure, there is an equilibrium between sea and land resistance. That rock which was once molten, now frozen in its inanimate torture, faces the constant pressure of sea waters crashing, welling in and falling back; and for the time being it seems fixed and indomitable. But the shore is altered by the displacement of each stone, or the tiniest splinter of rock. It is exposed not only to the assault of storm waves and surf, but of ice in some places, and of the sun, wind, and rain. The shore also has its dynamics in the life that has developed there, and its gradations over the various levels of that narrow zone where the two elements of salt water and air are forever meeting. It is a region of transition, of accommodation in the midst of battle.

The active principle of the shore is endless formation and destruction, change and variation; to see it at work is to understand the fluid combinations that make a landscape or a "scene." An ideal and probably impossible way for most of us to realize all this is to travel the shore from one end to the other. Still, an indicated journey, beginning in the far northern tip of Labrador and progressing to the Hudson River, may offer some clues.

Labrador stretches from its northernmost point opposite Baffin Island to the narrow Strait of Belle Isle which separates it from Newfoundland. It has a lonely shoreline of offshore islands, rocky ledges, dark and distant vistas, with great sweeps of tundra behind, as well as low bleak mountains and thousands of miles of spruce forests, countless lakes and streams. At its narrowest, the Strait of Belle Isle is only about nine miles across, yet the difference between Labrador to the north and Newfoundland to the south is very marked. Labrador is a region of savage extremes. It lies covered with snow for a large part of the year, but can be very warm during the summer. By comparison, the temperatures of Newfoundland, a great island surrounded by the sea, are relatively moderate. Its January average, in many areas, is in the low twenties, and for July somewhat less than sixty degrees. But Newfoundland is hardly mild as compared with Cape Cod or New York, with its late spring, its short summer, and the many raw and sudden changes that occur during the winter as westerly storms come raging out of the interior of the continent or northerly ones out of Hudson Bay, often in conflict. In the spring, and as late as July, gleaming icebergs, broken off the Greenland ice cap, come by the Newfoundland coast, sailing slowly and majestically on the tides, sometimes as much as a hundred feet high, flat-topped, or spiralled to a peak like the stylized carving of a flame.

Newfoundland abounds in boulder-strewn beaches at the head of narrow bays and coves, where isolated fishing settlements have existed on and off for five centuries, and where the Beothuk Indians had been coming for thousands of years before that. Its soils are acid, shallow, and stony for the most part, and, where the growing season is so short, agriculture is possible only on a small scale. On the other hand, as Newfoundland is rich in the berries of its bogs and tundra during the summer, it is also rich in the sea, whose shining and stormy surfaces have affected its whole character and the life of its people. For an inshore fisherman, this is an abundance which can vary along the coast to a frustrating degree, refusing him fish when he needs it most; and yet, sooner or later, the fish return. Except for a slight warming of the ocean waters in this century, and the resulting migration of some cold-water species northward, the conditions still prevail that were responsible for the fertility in marine life which was so impressive to Cartier and Cabot, though for reasons totally unknown to them.

The causes for the great proliferation of the "sacred" cod off Newfoundland are to be found in the geography of that island and its offshore banks, the circulation of the ocean waters, and the links between the living things of the sea. Out of the Arctic flows that cold, massive, sluggish but steadily moving system of waters known as the Labrador Current. Hugging the northeastern shore, it reaches south to Newfoundland, or even farther, before it loses force and is deflected eastward by the Gulf Stream. Where it flows over the Grand Banks off Newfoundland, this current comprises a broad band about five hundred miles across, and in the sunlight of spring its upwelling waters provide the mineral nutrients for a tremendous growth of the microscopic drifting sea life known as plankton. Fed by the phosphates and nitrates it carries, the diatoms flourish like a sea pasture, providing food for shrimps and other minute organisms which are in turn eaten by sea herring. The herring consume vast numbers of these planktonic animals, though not, it could be added, indiscriminately. Their gill rakers do not have the function of straining random quantities of food, but instead prevent food from escaping, and the herring show definite choice as to their prey, pursuing small organisms selectively. It is here that the voracious cod enters the scene, for though it eats all sorts and conditions of food, from shellfish to squid, the herring are especially to its liking. The cod's oceanic greed is matched by its fertility, one female spawning as many as four million eggs. So the fisheries which have made Newfoundland a major port of call for centuries are there because of the nutrients of the Labrador Current, linking directly to diatoms, the small animals that feed on diatoms, and then to herring and cod.

Newfoundland, which may be called the first settled country in North America, with due respect to the Indians whose claims date farther back, has been relatively poor in the modern, economic sense. The most easterly part of the North American land mass except for Greenland, it has a direct link with an age that antedates technology. Its fishermen, hunters, and subsistence farmers, with a rooted humor and color of speech, used to build their own houses, churches, and boats. Cod, seal, salmon, lobster, herring, and whales were their foundation. Newfoundland still sends its salted and sun-dried fish to the Catholic nations of Europe and to the Caribbean, and fishermen from Portugal, Spain, Norway, and Japan are still to be seen in its streets. But the old schooners that used to fish the Grand Banks are gone, as are the graceful white hulls and tall masts of the Portuguese sailing ships, once so common in the harbor of St. John. Modern trawlers are fishing intensively offshore, and the old, local, inshore fisheries can barely hold their own. Efforts are being made to exploit more of the land's mineral and timber resources in the interior. New roads are being built, and welfare checks help bridge the gap between an isolated but self-sufficient past and a future surely more involved.

For a man who knew how to fish in season, gather berries in the summer, and shoot caribou in fall and winter, bartering some of his produce for flour at the store, Newfoundland provided enough subsistence, in spite of its scanty soil and rough climate. Still, this island, some six thousand miles in circumference, would provide a poor living without its fish. Newfoundland has relatively few land animals, probably because of its geographical isolation rather than its climate. There have been no snakes or turtles on the island, and the green frog did not occur naturally but was introduced. The native mammals include only these few—beaver, muskrat, meadow mouse, little brown bat, long-eared bat, black bear, Arctic hare, and woodland caribou. Polar bear and Arctic fox show up periodically, rafted down from the north on floating ice, but are soon shot. These other mammals have been introduced, either accidentally or purposely—the common shrew, mink, house mouse, Norway rat, eastern chipmunk, snowshoe hare, and moose. This list is very short, far exceeded by mainland Labrador.

To the west and south of Newfoundland, in those islands that border on the Gulf of St. Lawrence, there is an essential difference in the landscape. In Newfoundland one has the sense of a whole country bound by fog-laden waters, a rugged, wild land of rocky coasts and fjords, inland marshes, innumerable lakes and ponds, of many wrinkled mountains, a place where man and his natural environment confront each other directly. On the Gaspé Peninsula of Quebec, or along the Gulf coast of New Brunswick, however, there are narrow fields divided by hedgerows sloping down to the water, a reminder of England, Ireland, or France. Prince Edward Island, cradled by the sweeping shores of Nova Scotia and New Brunswick, is given over to potatoes and forage for pigs and dairy cows; beyond its scalloped shoreline, bordered by strips of rich red soil, everything is deeply green, and the houses and barns are reminiscent of the New England countryside. A sense of isolation still lingers in many of these areas, the remnants of an older history, a land that subdued the people who inhabited it. Even the television antennae on the roofs seem a surface intrusion on lives lacking in modern speed and frenzy. The houses still have space between them. The speech of the people is soft, and suggests its recent ancestry in Europe.

In many regions of New Brunswick and Nova Scotia, the pillaging of spruce forests still goes on at an accelerating rate. Stand on the shore where the gray Atlantic rolls in, and it takes some feat of imagination to believe that to the west a whole continent of trees has already been cut down. Still, something of the primeval Canadian wilderness is intact, along with the cold roar of the sea, the winds, and the tides. The Canadian jay, or "whiskey jack," jumps stiffly down from the trees to cock an eye at the traveler. Wild woodland robins fly low and fast through the trees. Here, still, are long salmon rivers where the sunlight makes the water tremble and shimmer as it runs over small stones, and smaller streams impounded by beaver dams, and woodland banks beside them where deer walk down out of spruce and maple. The leaves of the maples fall across the surface of the water and are carried on, reflecting in multitudinous mirrors and yellow circles of light. Acadian chickadees, shyer than their black-capped relatives, send their wispy calls through the spruce, and an occasional bald eagle sails overhead.

The Gulf of St. Lawrence area is one of variety and marked transitions. In less than an hour a road from the highlands of Cape Breton, Nova Scotia, will take you down from a forest of almost pure fir at an altitude of a thousand feet, to a sandy shore littered with the shells of clams, moon snails, and scallops. The eastern shores of Nova Scotia are rocky; on the west the shoreline gives way to wide tidal flats gleaming with red mud at low tide. There are extensive salt marshes and tidal flats on one part of the coast —cliffs and stony beaches on the other—and the temperature of inshore waters varies from icy to cold to moderate.

At the right speed, that of a slow boat offshore, the extent of the Canadian coast and its detail are better seen, depending on the vagaries of marine weather. Everywhere are numerous low, spruce-covered islands, as well as huge boulders planted across the shallow waters of bays and harbors like stepping stones. Islands denuded of trees may be brown and rounded like mushroom tops, or, with a good growth of grass, like clumps of moss. Stony fields slope down to the shore. Over the water the sailor rounds one indefinite corner after another, seeing no more at times than the tips of spruce trees above a bank of soft gray fog rimmed on the horizon, as he cuts across a green sea intricate with wreaths and ripples, a cold sway of air and sea for the lungs, a sea-determined direction and atmosphere. At intervals through the fog, and when it lifts, there are cut-throughs and vistas toward the land in the form of salt marshes, wide bays, and deep inlets—an almost loose and floating landscape.

Down the northeast coast from Canada there are regional climates with variations and transitions like the land itself. Both northern Newfoundland and Quebec, including the Gaspé Peninsula, have a sub-Arctic climate. The rest of Newfoundland is more tempered by maritime influences, and from Nova Scotia southward the humidity is also higher and the summers cooler. In Nova Scotia and Maine the bitter cold of a continental winter is more obvious than on Cape Cod, though both lie along the sea. The area along Long Island Sound, west of Rhode Island, has the same general type of climate, which has been described as humid-continental, but the summers there are often much hotter and more humid than along the coast of Massachusetts.

In the St. Lawrence region of Canada the war of influence between maritime and continental weather is such that the winds seem to come in from every direction at once. Fog, rain, humidity —moisture in all its aspects—affect it throughout the year. The restlessness and changeability of the climate is allied to the sea, although extremes are still greater to the south where the temperature may rise or drop twenty or thirty degrees within a few hours during a shifting season.

In spite of all the wet dull days, the long cold lulls between one season and another, the empty monotony of gray waters offshore, the months and months of leafless trees and colorless ground, the whole year rocks and moves from one new action to another, a balance of interacting forces from land and sea.

There are many places where the great natural energies that give the coast its character are clearly seen, but none more so than where tidal lands border the Bay of Fundy between Nova Scotia and New Brunswick. The bay has the greatest known rise and fall of tides in the world—at one of its arms, the Minas Basin in Nova Scotia, the tidal range can amount to forty or fifty feet. The arrival of the incoming tide up the inlet at Windsor is an impressive sight. At the start it is manifested as a mere rushing in of a thin band of muddy water across a river bed gleaming with wet mud and shallows. But in no more than ten minutes the water begins to rise; the pools expand and then merge as the waters flow in on various levels. Along the banks, water currents flow downstream again as the river basin fills, and they meet the tidal waters coming up. There is an intermingling, a synchronization of water forces, first covering the middle reaches and then rising up the sides, until the whole wide bed fills in.

Minas Basin forms one branch of the Bay of Fundy at its northern end, and Chignecto Bay, with an inlet from the Petitcodiac River, provides the other. Up this river is the famous "Bore," best seen in the town of Moncton, New Brunswick, where the times of its arrival are posted daily in the city street. Below Moncton the inrushing tides of the Bay of Fundy force a tremendous volume of water through the river's gradually narrowing neck. Thus confined, the tidal wave becomes radically steepened, and it advances as a wall of water. Its height is not great as compared with similar phenomena in other parts of the world—it is about three feet as a

rule, occasionally rising to five or six feet—and some find it un-
exciting. But as it approaches, on time like most trains, with a
rushing, roaring sound, and gulls shift to the sides of the river to
escape it, anyone viewing it for the first time might feel that it had
an almost uncanny, inexorable power.

Viewed from high in the air, or as seen on a relief map, the
coast that begins south of the Bay of Fundy looks folded, craggy,
and uneven, as rough as a broad area of bark through which rivers
and streams run like open veins and arteries, reflecting a sky as
blue as the watery wilderness they join. This rocky coast of
Maine, with the islands in its various bays looking like so many
wood chips scattered across the water, is so irregular as to con-
found our sense of distance. A bay that may be crossed by boat in
a matter of minutes may take more than an hour to round by
road. On a map the direct distance between Maine's southern and
northern boundaries is seen to be only about 230 miles, but along
a line tracing all the inlets, coves, and bays, the distance stretches
to some 3,750 miles. Even the coastline of Massachusetts, though
much less irregular than that of Maine, is about 2,200 miles when
measured in and out, in its entirety, although the direct length is
only 192 miles. Travelers by boat can easily lose their bearings
among Maine's countless islands, with their surf-whitened ledges
and jagged rocks covered with scarfs of golden rockweed swinging
easily in the tides.

One of the first of these islands to be charted was Monhegan,
whose steep seaward-facing cliffs are exposed to the full force of
storm waves from the open Atlantic. During such storms the spray
may cover the spruce that crown the cliff known as White Head a
hundred feet above the sea. To early sailors and fishermen
Monhegan was a familiar landfall with a haven on its protected
side. In the year 1605, the explorer George Weymouth described
it as "woody, growen with Firre, Oke, and Beach, as farre as we
saw along the shore. . . . The water issued forth down the Rocky

Cliffes in many places; and much fowle of divers kinds breed upon the shore and rocks." Inland he found "excellent mould" of soil, and rivers with salmon leaping above water.

To the eye of the geologist, the irregularity of the Maine coast, a land seemingly afloat in the sea, tells its own story. It shows that this is a drowned land, that the inlets are the flooded mouths of rivers, the islands actually the summits of hills and mountains that once rose above the coastal plain. The Bay of Fundy itself is a drowned river valley, the channel so deeply submerged and overwhelmed by the inflowing sea that it now lies many fathoms beneath the surface. North of Cape Cod, what in a past geologic age was a broad, comparatively level coastal plain dotted with peaks, is also totally submerged.

The rise and fall of sea and land with respect to each other is a complex phenomenon, taking place over great stretches of time, but what we see today on the coast of Maine is unmistakably the result of the most recent ice age. In it two primary forces were at work. The colossal frozen masses of ice, a mile high in some places, impounded an immense amount of the world's supply of water, bringing the level of the sea much lower than it is today and uncovering the coastal plain as dry land. But the massive weight of the ice had another effect as well—the crust of the earth buckled under its weight, tilting seaward all along the coast. Then as the ice melted, the sea level rose, flooding the sunken region to such a depth that its whole aspect was transformed. The land has sprung back sufficiently from the weight of the ice so that marine deposits have been found far inland in Maine, and there are other indications of old shorelines to be seen above sea level.

The sea which now laps against the rocks of the Maine coast has not appreciably eroded them, although it may have hollowed out the base of a cliff, helped boulders round each other, pummeled and enlarged small caves, or accelerated the normal cracking and sundering of the rock structure over several thousand years. For one thing the components of these ledges sloping into the sea are mainly "hard rocks," such as quartzite, gneiss, schist, or slate. For another, there simply has not been enough time. For the past 4,000 years or so the sea has stood at approximately the same position in relation to the land—not much more time than to scratch the surface of this resistant rock. Many millions of years were needed to wear down the interior New England upland to its present state, a relatively level plain with here and there a resistant mass such as Mount Monadnock in New Hampshire or Mount Graylock in Massachusetts. On some of the "soft rock" shores, weaker sandstones and glacial deposits have been considerably eroded, particularly those most exposed to the sea; but even they have not receded very far, or changed very much, compared with the changes that will come in the future. It is all a matter of time.

Eventually the sea will change this young coast by a gradual cutting away, turning slopes into cliffs, with sand bars formed offshore, and inland streams carrying down debris to fill in lagoons behind them, until all the kinks and jagged edges of the shoreline have been worn away. When that happens, the coast will have reached a stage of maturity. That stage is beginning to be reached along the coast south of Portland, Maine. The inroads of time and the sea upon the shorelines of Cape Ann and Cape Cod have not been in progress any longer than those upon the headlands of Maine; the difference lies in the character of the weaker rocks, which have reached a greater degree of frontal regularity in the same length of time. Yet, already, the straight line of cliffs along the Outer Beach of Cape Cod, cut by the sea out of a sloping plain that began as a mass of stony debris dumped by the glaciers, may be called a mature shoreline.

South of Portland, the islands and the long peninsulas reaching into the sea begin to be succeeded by curving, though still rocky, shores, with shallow coves and gray crescent beaches, with an increasing number of offshore shoals, and barrier beaches of sand spits enclosing marshes behind them. More and more, the boulders, ledges, and shingle alternate with more sandy beaches. The marshes, of all sizes and extent, are often the only open areas left, like pocket oases among the small beach cities, cities of the summertime, and the roads, the refuse, and the litter. Our insistence on a featureless landscape is not peculiar to the twentieth century. Boston, for example, used to be a region covered with low, dome-like or egg-shaped hills moulded by the glaciers and known as drumlins, intersected by a network of tidal channels and marshes. Long before the present century these hills were dug away, and the material used to fill in coves, marshes, and valleys to make the city an integral part of the coast. Some of the drumlins still rise like the backs of whales out of Boston Harbor. Bunker and Breed's hills are both drumlins; but most of their kind vanished under the concrete and asphalt.

For all their levelling, these shores are still imbued with a subtlety denied to their exploiters. Storm waves take away beach heads and low cliffs, altering the shoreline. On Cape Cod's great Outer Beach, the erosion of the cliffs goes on at the rate of three to four feet a year, the displaced sand being carried away by offshore currents and returned to build new land at Provincetown and on Monomoy Island. In the same way, stretches of shore along the more protected reaches of Cape Cod Bay are added to and subtracted from by storm waves and currents over the years. There is an ebb and flow in the physiography of the shore down its entire length.

The partially submerged shores south of Maine have all been formed out of glacial debris, material that can be eroded fairly easily by the waves, and shifted from place to place by the currents. Cape Cod, Nantucket, Martha's Vineyard, and Long Island are almost entirely the work of glaciers, a mixture of clay, stones, and boulders resting on submerged banks.

Traveling south from Cape Cod, the pitch pines and stunted oaks begin to be replaced by larger oaks, white pines, red maples, and willows in marshy inland ground, and by scattered clumps of juniper across stony fields. Bays and rivers intersect along the coast. Buzzards Bay and Westport in Massachusetts, Sakonnet and Narragansett in Rhode Island, and then the coast of Connecticut are entered by river after river flowing southward into salt water. An outwash plain along the Rhode Island coast and into Connecticut slopes broadly down to the shore where long sandbars protect salt ponds and inland marshes. There are numerous small rivers, as well as the large ones with cities astride them, like New London on the Thames, Old Saybrook and Old Lyme perched on either side of the Connecticut, New Haven on the Quinnipiac, Bridgeport on the Housatonic.

Along the north shores of Long Island Sound, low undulating hills descend to a long series of stony or gravely beaches, between which rise low sea walls built by man to protect houses and streets from storm waves. Across the sound lies fish-shaped Long Island, touching New York City at its western tip, and the two lobes of its tail jutting eastward into the Atlantic. The upper lobe of the tail, Orient Point, is a morainal ridge, debris left by the last glacier; and the lower, Montauk, was left behind by an earlier advance of the glacier. Northern Long Island shores are rocky, though cut with beaches; along the southern shore, which faces the Atlantic, lie the dunes and sandy stretches of an outwash plain. Small rivers flow through marshes or under the shade of oak, maple, and hickory, and on the south shore there are wide areas of salt marsh behind superb barrier beaches. Bottlenose dolphins arch through the waters of the sound during many months of the year. Local fishermen troll for porgy, fluke, and summer or winter flounder there, or cast for sea bass along the Great South Beach on Fire Island. A variety of birds have found niches in the pitch pine barrens and hardwood forests, along the edge of fields cleared for potatoes and cabbages, as well as in the marshes and by the shore. Much that was once naturally abundant on Long Island, past present conceiving, is now gone. Much else, through valiant effort, has been preserved, and, as of 1964, Fire Island has become a federal responsibility as a National Seashore.

Like a funnel, Long Island Sound, and an ever-crowding complex of human habitation and industry that border it and narrow it down, leads into the vast blocks and towers of New York. The waters of the sound join the East River, which has Manhattan Island on one side, Brooklyn and Queens on the other, and then merge with the wide Hudson in the teeming expanse of the harbor, flowing south into the Upper Bay, and finally through the Narrows to empty into the Atlantic Ocean.

The lower Hudson, like the many small tidal rivers and inlets of Maine, is a drowned river valley, and the hills of Staten Island and lower Brooklyn that border it are part of the same terminal moraine that forms the backbone of Long Island, in which the Narrows itself is but a breach, kept open by the flood that pours out of the Hudson. Underwater mapping has revealed that the Hudson's deep-walled, winding, submarine canyon beyond the coastline is comparable to some of the most spectacular canyons on land. This canyon is a continuation of the rocky bed of the Hudson, which attains great depths long before the river arrives at its outlet in the sea. At the Storm King Highlands, not quite fifty miles upstream from Manhattan, the Hudson deepens to about 950 feet, then it becomes relatively shallow until it flows into the offshore channel, where it plunges as deep as 6,600 feet over the continental shelf.

Of the many places along the shore from Labrador to Long Island whose present estate contrasts with what we know of their primeval majesty, none is more striking—or appalling—than the mouth of the Hudson River. In 1609, when Henry Hudson sailed up the river in his two-master, the *Half Moon*, the explorers found

Manna-hata Island "indented with bays, coves, and creeks" that no longer exist. Probably more than a hundred brooks were "pleasant and proper for man and beast to drink, as well as agreeable to behold." Some of those brooks still flow underneath the concrete veneer of the island inside large diameter pipes or as part of the city's sewage system. In many places, notably to the north of what is now Times Square, there was a forest of tremendous oaks, with open grassy glades where land had been burned off for agriculture by the Indians. The Indian trails that interlaced the region survive today, if at all, as the car-jammed lanes of Broadway. What was once a marsh-bordered stream is now Canal Street. Where deer raced through the trees, shoppers now thread their way among the stores of Fifth Avenue; and where birds were so abundant that "whoever is not lazy can catch them with little difficulty," there are now close-ranked towers of steel and glass. Where once pure waters yielded up their bounty of shellfish, and sturgeon ran up the river, pollution has long since done its work. The lobsters were all gone by the beginning of the nineteenth century, and where the ten-inch oysters once thrived, the beds that are left have been poisoned beyond redemption.

Nature, which is not absent from any part of the earth, is still to be found in New York City within the spreading knot of human power. Migratory birds still pause over Central Park, and some shad are still left in the Hudson; winter winds still howl through the concrete canyons as they once did through the columns of forest trees. But like all great cities, it has become the kind of place where men can concentrate on themselves almost to the exclusion of every other form of life.

# SHORE PATTERNS

**3**

A NARROW, SHIFTING RIBBON marks the encounter between sea and land. Though the boundaries of the shore may be defined as the lowest and the highest reaches of the tides, who can say where the sea begins or ends? Far offshore, beyond the lowest tideline, the sea is still affected by the land beneath, by its slope and composition; and even farther out, the land is implicit in the currents and the winds that send the waves crashing home. Likewise, on land, beyond the highest reaches of the tide itself, lies a zone that is moistened daily at high tide by the falling droplets of the spray—and beyond that is still another reached now and then by the spray when storm waves are high. Even farther inland the sea makes its presence known in humidity, wind, and fog.

Nor can the shores from Labrador to the mouth of the Hudson River be defined in terms of physical composition alone. Some general statements have been made about the prevalence of rocky shores north of Portland, Maine, but even there the visitor will find an occasional stretch of firm sand, loose pebbles, marsh, or mud-flat among the jutting rocks of its headlands and coves. The un-ending conflict between sea and land means that for every place where an equilibrium between sea and land is to be found, there will be another where the ceaseless movement of the waves and the tides is undoing that same equilibrium.

Nevertheless, the shore as a habitat for living things is marked by certain broad patterns—of composition, of climate, of tides and currents, and of the living things themselves. Shore habitats may be variously classified, but perhaps the most convenient sub-division is that of composition—whether they are predominantly rock, pebbles, sand, or mud. One by one, each of these habitats will be looked at more closely in the chapters that follow. For now, it is sufficient to note that all of them ultimately derive from rock; it is the size of the particles that makes the difference.

A solid base of rock gives support to a luxuriant growth of seaweeds with their rootlike holdfasts, and to a variety of inver-tebrates—barnacles, mussels, snails, sea anemones, starfish—such as can cement themselves to the rocks or cling there by means of suction organs. A shore where shattered rock fragments and water-smoothed pebbles are jarred and tumbled and abraded by the constant overturning of the waves gives little shelter for life, and is usually barren. Sand gives little support to seaweeds and none to animals such as barnacles, and on a sandy shore much of the life is hidden from view; beneath the surface, sand affords shelter to a large population of burrowing animals such as are usually absent from rocky shores—worms, certain mollusks, and crustaceans. A muddy shore is usually one sheltered against the full force of the waves, and in its fertile layers plants take root—such as the underwater forests of the eelgrass, where certain kinds of starfishes, sea cucumbers (wormlike relatives of the starfish) and worms, quite different from those that inhabit the sandy beach, are at home.

The visitor to any of these coasts can see how the stark physical conditions affect the lives of plants and animals, and how these in turn affect the physical environment. The seaweeds, for example, are found primarily on rocky shores where they can anchor themselves; but such is the complexity of their interrelation with the shore that they shelter and preserve the rocks against the full force of waves, insulating them against sudden changes of temperature that would otherwise fracture them and hasten their disintegration. Thus each part of the shore has to be defined in many ways: temperatures, tidal heights and depths, composition of the substratum, relative salinities, the presence or absence of certain kinds of life, among others. And within each portion of the shore, a cross-cut from sea to dry land reveals another range of complexities, from areas that are uncovered only for a very short time at the lowest tides to those above high tide that are reached only by the spray.

Man is a systematizer and organizer of facts, and his understanding often increases with the patterns he can detect. Of the numerous broad patterns of environment along the shore, of response to it and to each other by living things, a book of this size can touch upon only the most fundamental. Perhaps the first of these is the pattern imposed by climate. The multitudes of living things at the shore are usually in delicate adjustment to the prevailing climate, so much so that even a change too slight for human senses to detect can be a disaster. Unless it can find shelter under a seaweed or in a crevice, a brittle star dies when the temperature of the shallow water in its tidepool climbs toward one hundred degrees. Most inhabitants of the shore similarly display only a limited tolerance for such changes, but there are exceptions: the horseshoe crab, which can survive freezing in the New England ice, is of the same species that basks in the tepid waters of Florida.

Plants and animals that inhabit the shores along the Bay of Fundy must cope with great tidal changes and with cold water. Oysters are not usually found in the Bay of Fundy, because they require fairly high summer temperatures, upward of 68° F., for spawning—preferably in a partly enclosed bay or estuary with brackish water. Some oyster beds are close to Canadian shores, mostly in the southern half of the Gulf of St. Lawrence; otherwise they are exceedingly rare above Boston and Cape Cod, and along the Atlantic shore they do not become truly abundant until the warmer waters of Chesapeake Bay.

Since most plants and animals are bound to the prevailing climate of the shore, it is possible to divide the narrow, twisting band of shore along the northeastern coast into zones of life. Far to the north is the Arctic Zone, where the growth of plant plankton is seasonal but may be enormous, and where the fish that feed on it may thrive for short periods. These shores are limited in the kinds of plants and animals they can support, and even those animals must be able to emigrate from the harshness of the winter ice, as many kinds of fishes do, or be able to live under it, as do the polar cod and certain seals.

Labrador and northern Newfoundland form a zone known as the sub-Arctic; its southern boundary may be defined as the farthest penetration of floating ice. Below the sub-Arctic, the chill, southward-flowing Labrador Current bathes a region where the cold is less extreme—the Boreal Province between southern Newfoundland and the northern shore of Cape Cod. Biologically this is the richest portion of the northeastern shore, because its jagged coves offer a wide range of habitats and because many species can find suitable living conditions in the heavy growth of seaweed.

The flexed arm of Cape Cod, reaching fifty miles into the Atlantic, is a sort of biological dividing line. It separates the cold waters to the north from the warmer waters, moderated by the Gulf Stream, to the south. To the north of the cape are found typical plants and animals of the Boreal Province; to the south, in what is called the Transatlantic Province, there are mixed populations of warm-water species in the summer, cold-water species in winter.

The temperature of the water just north of the cape, on an annual average, is about ten degrees cooler than on the southern side. A difference of ten degrees may not appear to be important, but it may greatly affect adult shore animals, and also prevent the young animals from surviving. In some places the distance across the cape that separates the cool and warm waters is only about a mile, yet it marks a greater difference in the distribution of living things than there is, for example, between Martha's Vineyard and the Virginia coast, nearly five hundred miles to the south. There are many cold-water species of marine invertebrates that are found on both sides of the cape but do not breed to the south of it, except, like the dog whelk, in the dead of winter, and others like fiddler crabs and blue crabs which can be found along Cape Cod Bay but not to the north beyond a distance as close as Boston. The bay scallop frequents warm, shallow bays on the north side of the cape, but is much more prevalent to the south. The green sea urchin is common north of Cape Cod up to the tide pools of Maine and Canada but is not much found on its south side except in deeper waters.

A study several decades ago of forty species of marine invertebrates common along the northeastern coast showed that sixteen ranged no farther north than the cape and fourteen no farther south; there were ten others that occurred on both sides of the cape. During the past forty or fifty years, Cape Cod has become less of a boundary. A warming trend in the northern part of the globe appears to have allowed several southern species to survive and reproduce north of the cape. The green crab, a predator on clams, was once found only south of the cape, but early in this century it extended its range; it has now spread as far north as Nova Scotia. Several species of fishes found near shore— menhaden, round herring, and whiting, for example—that once were totally absent or very scarce north of the cape, today are often caught along the Gulf of Maine. At the same time, cool-water species such as the cod have been deserting the warming waters just north of the cape, and the center of the cod's abundance has now shifted far northward to Greenland.

All of the zones from the Arctic to the Transatlantic, and the life in each one, are affected in various ways by another pattern of change along the shore, the ceaseless ebb and flow of the tides. There is, of course, great variation in tidal ranges and effects, not only at specific places but also at different phases of the moon. The relative ranges of the tides along the shore can have their effects on its topography, especially in regions where the material is loose and malleable. Thus the amplitude of the tides on the north side of Cape Cod has produced extensive marshes and wide sandy flats, whereas on its south side, where the tidal reach is lower, there are small, sheltered bays, narrow beaches, and much smaller marsh areas. On a rocky coast the effects of high and low tide are written on the rocks, exposed and covered daily to varying degrees; on a sandy shore the life burrows underground, and the work of the tide is seen only in a wetted surface and the presence or absence of ripple marks.

The tides are a complex phenomenon; but in general they are caused by the gravitational pull of the moon, and to a lesser extent of the sun, upon the waters of the revolving earth. Twice each month, when their reach is greatest, they are called "spring" tides —a reference not to the season but to the way the water at those times appears to spring up onto the land. As a result of physical laws too complex to be explained except in mathematical terms, spring tides occur a few days after the moon is full and again after it is new. At the time of new moon, the moon and the sun are in a direct line on the same side of the earth, so that their gravitational pull is combined; at the time of full moon, when the earth lies directly between the sun and the moon, the pull is combined once again. The lowest tides—known as the "neap," probably from an ancient Norse word meaning "scarcely touching"—occur when the moon is in its first and third quarters, appearing in the sky as a half moon. At those times the sun and the moon are at right angles to the earth, and, since each somewhat counteracts the pull of the other, the rise and fall of the tides are not so great. Although this simplified explanation applies to tides in general, the tides at any particular stretch of shore may become exceedingly complex. Tides from different parts of the ocean may join forces and amplify each other to produce extremely high water, or one may neutralize the other to produce a small tidal range.

Tides are extremely important in determining the character of the coast against which their waters strike, and of the animals and plants that can live there. The mean range of the tide at the island of Nantucket is about one and a half feet; at the Bay of Fundy it may be fifty feet. The tides on the southern side of Cape Cod have a range of about two feet, but on the bay shore they average about ten feet. North of Cape Cod, where the tides come under the influence of the Bay of Fundy, they gradually increase in range, to a dozen feet at Bar Harbor on Mount Desert Island, on up to twenty two at Calais on the Maine–New Brunswick border. Such a wide range of pulsations is due to many factors— the topography of the sea floor, the local currents, and also the numerous irregularities of the coastline. The tidal movement originates in the ocean; as it reaches the coast, the configuration of each individual bay, inlet, and headland has its own peculiar effect upon tidal elevations and intervals in any given area. The tide-producing forces of the sun and the moon in themselves have very little effect on the waters of a river. But as the tides of the sea move up the estuaries of the St. Lawrence, the Connecticut, the Hudson, and dozens of smaller rivers, great water masses are transported inland. According to the mathematics of tidal phenomena, these masses are affected in their rate of speed by the width of the river, the character of its banks, and the depth of its channel. At one time the power of the incoming tide was harnessed to turn the wheels of water mills, which until the beginning of the last century were numerous along the northeastern shore.

The endless changes of the tides greatly affect the plants and animals of the shore. Perhaps the most obvious influence is the gradation of moisture—from the total wetness of the sea to intermittent drenchings and dryings, to moistenings now and then or perhaps not at all. A small stretch of rocky Maine shore may appear a more or less uniform environment, but closer inspection reveals that for the creatures that inhabit it the tides have marked off numerous zones, each with its own set of conditions. To the landward, there is first of all the inland area that is never reached even by the spray from high storm waves. Between it and the sea is a zone that receives spray only at times of severe storms; closer still to the sea is another that receives spray even from ordinary storms. Next comes a zone that is moistened by wind-driven droplets from the highest tides, and next to it the innermost of the zones wetted by the tides themselves. This area is covered by water only twice each month, at the time of the highest spring tides. Still farther down the shore and nearer to the sea are, first, the zone covered at mean high water of the spring tides, then one covered at the highest of the neap tides, and so on down to the shore's lowest zone, the one that remains under water even when tides are at their lowest.

There is no living thing at the shore that is not in some way affected by the twice-daily advance of the sea against the ramparts of the land. For each of the tidal animals, the ebbing of the tide brings periodically a brief but threatening experience of living in a waterless world. For those that live near the low-tide line, the complete exposure to sun and wind is brief, though nevertheless critical to their survival; for those that live above the reaches even of wind-driven spray, where wetting is only occasional, the requirements are rigorous. The tides change from day to day and even from minute to minute, and as they change they have many effects on the life at the shore. They bring changes in the temperature and the salinity of the water; they pull some organisms out to sea and transport the young of some, such as barnacles, to their habitats high up on the beach. The fall of the tides means exposure to drying wind and sun, and their rise means that plants and animals must have evolved ways to resist the pounding and pressure of the oncoming waters.

In general, the higher up on the shore that an animal lives, the more efficiently it must protect itself against drying out. For barnacles this is quite easy; they simply close the plates of their hard shells, thus retaining some of the moisture of the sea inside. Snails retreat into their shells and close the doorlike operculum; some also secrete an airtight mucus across the shell opening to keep from drying out until the return of the next tide. Some animals, such as worms, burrow into the moist areas left by the ebbing tide; some species of crabs that cannot themselves burrow are able to use the burrows of other shore animals. Finally, there are animals—certain starfishes and beachfleas are just two out of many—that neither burrow nor possess shells in which to find sanctuary but that are highly mobile; as the tide retreats they find temporary pools of water, thick mats of moist seaweed, or shaded crevices in rocks.

As the rising tide moves farther up the beach, many of the creatures that have lain dormant or protected in burrows and crevices awaken in a feverish burst of activity. The inward sweep of the tide carries with it an abundance of food, and to capture it shore animals open their shells or seine the water with strange feeding tubes and tentacles; predators such as starfishes and whelks move about, claiming their share of food from among the harvesters themselves. Many shore animals respond to the tide's advance not only because it brings them food but because their whole way of life is adapted to it. The barnacles that live near the high-tide line must wait for tides to bring them food and moisture, and also to carry away the young that will colonize new shores. The common periwinkle, which in some places lives above the high-tide line, appears to be nearly independent of the sea; yet it still must await the coming of the spring tides to carry away its eggs. Some worms, on the other hand, adjust their spawning to the neap rather than to the spring tides, since the latter would sweep the larvae too far from the places favorable to their growth.

The tides are only one of the stirrings of the sea that shape the life along its shores. Still more dramatic is the movement of the waves. Two centuries ago the waves at Cape Cod were described by Jean de Crèvecoeur in his *Letters from an American Farmer*:

Who is the landsman that can behold without affright so singular an element, which by its impetuosity seems to be the destroyer of this poor planet, yet at particular times accumulates the scattered fragments and produces islands and continents fit for men to dwell on!

Cape Cod was, as it still is, an excellent place to note the effects of waves. Whereas the protected bay shores of the cape are extravagantly productive of life, the side facing the Atlantic is so endlessly attacked by surf, so endlessly changing and shifting, that plants and animals can scarcely take any permanent hold.

Authorities on the subject classify waves into several different kinds. Those of most interest to shore visitors, however, are the wind-caused movements that form into breakers as they approach the shore. Such a wave is not a volume of water moving shoreward. It is not the water itself that moves toward the shore, but rather the *shape* of the wave; as a wave advances, each particle of water in it rotates in a full circle and returns almost exactly to its original position. This effect can be seen by observing a piece of driftwood; it remains steadily in place, rising and falling with the motion of the water under it; when eventually it does reach the shore, it will have been carried there by wind and currents, not by waves. Because the prevailing winds in the North Atlantic are westerly, most of the waves produced by storms far out in the ocean eventually break on the shores of Europe; except for those tossed up by tropical hurricanes, the waves that roll in on North Atlantic coast are usually the work of storms fairly close to shore.

A wave is best visualized as a revolving cylinder of water which sets in motion another cylinder alongside it, and so on. The cylinders, as they rub against the increasingly shallow bottom near the shore, gradually change shape. Partly because of the friction against the bottom and partly as a result of complex mathematical laws governing the motion of waves, their revolutions become slower as the water becomes shallower. Since the front of the revolving cylinder is shallower than the back, it moves more slowly, until finally a point is reached at which the water particles at the back of the wave overtake those at the front. It is then that the crest falls forward, breaking the cylindrical motion of the wave into the foaming overturn of the surf.

Breakers differ from waves formed at sea in that they actually give forward momentum to the particles of water, so as to hurl immense volumes of water against the shore. The breaking of an incoming wave, though, is not necessarily the end of it. Energy not dissipated by the collapse of the cylinder may drive the water onward to reform into new, smaller waves still closer to shore. In many places along the steep, rocky coast of Maine, an irregular pattern of breakers may be seen, where even after the water has struck the shore, it may still contain enough energy to generate a new wave that moves seaward to meet the incoming waves. On many parts of the northeastern coast, it is not unusual for breakers to exert a pressure of some two tons per square foot, enough to hurl large boulders about as if they were bowling balls. Even this intense force may be amplified to an almost unbelievable degree when the mass of water shot from the crest of a breaking wave carries with it a trapped pocket of air, which is compressed and hurled against the shore. This shock pressure may last only a few hundredths of a second, but during that time it may exert an explosive force of eight tons per square foot. It is thus no wonder that at times waves have been a powerful agent in carving even the resistant rocks of the Maine shore, scooping out caves, undermining cliffs and causing them to collapse, splitting the smooth faces of rocks asunder.

Even the breakers of comparatively calm waters carry with them pebbles and sand, abrasive pellets that steadily bombard a rocky shore and have their long-run effect on its character and shape, though on coasts made of loose glacial material it is the storm waves that cause major changes. "I saw the play of the Atlantic with the coast," wrote Ralph Waldo Emerson in 1847, after a visit to Nantucket. "Every wave reached a quarter of a mile along shore as it broke. . . . Ah, what freedom and grace and beauty with all this might!" Now, little more than a century later, the places where Emerson stood may long since have disappeared into the sea. In one place on the south shore of Nantucket, measurements over a fourteen-year period revealed that the sea had been claiming an average of seventeen feet of land each year. It has been estimated that most of Cape Cod will be gone in another two thousand years, leaving only some shoals and a few of the higher and wider areas emergent above the sea, and that two thousand years after that even these will have disappeared utterly. The same fate is in prospect for the offshore islands of Martha's Vineyard and Nantucket. Not that all of this rock, sand, and mud will simply vanish. The currents will carry it elsewhere and deposit it along other shores, building up new beaches, new rolling dunes; in a way this is already happening, for Cape Cod Bay grows shallower every year, and new dry land is being built up near the tip of Cape Cod at Provincetown.

The lighthouses, cottages, and wharves, even the breakwaters that man builds along the coast, are often defenseless against the explosive power of waves. Still more helpless are the plants and animals at the shore under the bombardment of storms and the unending tides; to live at all under these conditions has called forth certain peculiar patterns of adjustment. The rocky coast affords opportunity for life to exist in two primary ways: by clinging and by dissipating the force of the waters. Sand, by contrast, is a shifting medium, with no opportunity for attachment, but with yielding particles that allow an animal to burrow below their unstable surface. A different set of adjustments is made where a sandy shore is protected against the full force of the waves by a peninsula or offshore islands. Even slight differences in the sizes of the mineral particles at a sandy beach may determine what can live there. If the beach is composed mainly of large, coarse particles that shift in the surf, the substratum not only is too unstable even for many kinds of burrowing animals, but also it dries out quickly; thus the only animals that can survive here are those that can dig deeply down to the area of constant wetness that is not disturbed by the swirling waters. Where a sandy beach is composed of very small particles that pack together firmly, it retains moisture after the retreat of the tides and is little disturbed by their return; although at low tide this kind of sandy beach may appear as barren as one made up of large particles, under the surface it is very much alive.

The clingers at the rocky shore include animals that remain attached to the rocks with the aid of cement, anchoring threads, and suction. Barnacles cement their shells to the rocks; also, the

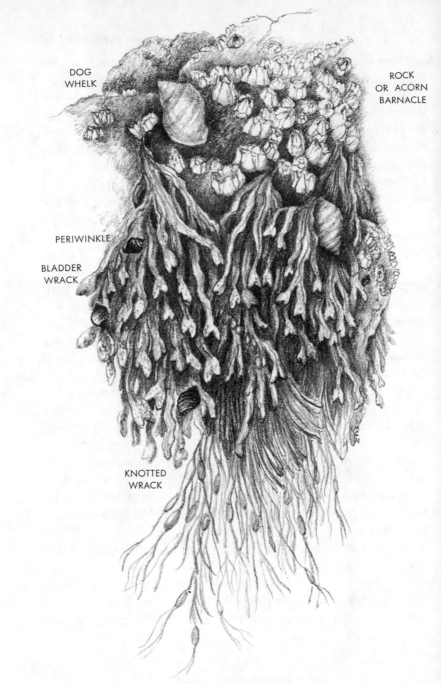

DOG
WHELK

ROCK
OR ACORN
BARNACLE

PERIWINKLE

BLADDER
WRACK

KNOTTED
WRACK

Detail of Rocky Shore

force of the water is dissipated by the streamlined shape of the shells. Mussels, instead of cementing themselves permanently to rocks, spin out a number of extraordinarily strong filaments that serve as anchor lines; even though a heavy surf may snap some of these, enough usually hold until the mussel can replace the rest. Even the seemingly vulnerable starfish can anchor itself in a heavy surf by means of multitudinous tube feet on its underside, each one ending in a suction disk. This low, flat animal is aided, too, by its shape: the blows of the waves, instead of dislodging it, actually press it down, reinforcing the grip of its suction disks on the rock.

The plants at the rocky shore have evolved exactly the same methods of survival: clinging and dissipating the energy of the surf. Many of the kelps, which live in the surf zone, grow structures known as holdfasts that somewhat resemble the roots of a tree as they branch and rebranch and find secure attachment to the rocks. Most of the kelps also have long fronds whose structure and chemical composition enable them to dissipate the force of the water. The acids and salts that compose the tissues of most kinds of kelp give the fronds a strong, leathery but elastic texture that enables them to endure the pounding of the surf. Some kinds, such as the horsetail kelp and winged kelp, are frayed into thin ribbons which offer little resistance to the pulling and tugging of the waters.

The climate, the tides, the waves and currents, the composition of the rock or sand, all go into the environment of living things at the shore. But no less important are the relations among the living things themselves. Other plants and animals are just as much a part of the environment as the rock the kelp clings to or the sand the worm burrows into. Of the numerous patterns of relationship among the creatures of the shore, none is more impressive than the food chain. In the economy of life along the shore, the relation between the eater and the eaten stands out clearly. The animal that feeds on a particular plant or animal is fed upon in turn by other animals. In almost any food chain, two facts are apparent: as the chain proceeds upward from stage to stage, the size of the predatory animal almost invariably increases; and the numbers of animals at the bottom of the chain are very much greater than at the top.

A sample food chain—reaching, let us say, from the microscopic plants known as diatoms to man—demonstrates these two facts. If the diatoms and the sequence of animals in the chain were measured, it would be seen that each time one organism captured and consumed another, there would be an energy loss of about nine-tenths. In other words, approximately ten pounds of prey are needed to add one pound to the animal that does the preying. Green plants are at the bottom of every food chain, for only they can harness the energy of the sun, by means of photosynthesis, and convert it into food. About 10,000 pounds of diatoms, the floating plants of the sea, are needed as food to make 1,000 pounds of the crustaceans that feed upon them; these small, shelled animals will, in turn, be fed upon by the small fish known as smelt, and a thousand pounds of them will produce about a hundred pounds of smelt. That hundred pounds of smelt, in turn, will be converted into ten pounds of mackerel, a larger fish, which will contribute one pound to the still larger tuna that devours it. And that pound of tuna finally will add a tenth of a pound to the weight of the man who makes a meal of it. Thus the path that leads from the primary producers of energy (the countless billions of minute diatoms) to the final consumer (the single human being) shows the ultimate survival of only a tenth of a pound out of the original resource at the beginning of the chain of 10,000 pounds.

This one example demonstrates the typical profligacy of life at the early stages of the food chains at the shore. A large oyster may produce half a billion eggs during the warm season; one medium-sized crab was found to be carrying 4,900,000 eggs. Of course not all the eggs of either will hatch, very few of the offspring will ever reach adulthood, and fewer still will ever reproduce. Yet this prodigality, this sheer wastage of life, gives great importance to the competition for space. In every environment on the globe there is some competition for living and feeding space; but nowhere can it be seen more clearly than at the rocky shore.

Much of the life there is sedentary, not only because of the rocks that can be clung to, but also because it is not necessarily an advantage to be able to move about so long as food is swept shoreward by the tides. But a rock, even a many-faceted one, offers only so much space to cling to, and most of the animals seeking that space lose out to myriads of competitors, both of their own and of other species with the same needs. The competition for space is mainly among young animals looking for a place to settle; but even after this first weeding out the struggle continues, the weaker ones crowded out by the stronger. Where a rock is so closely covered with barnacles that the cones of their shells touch, there is obviously little chance for new larval-stage colonists; any young barnacle that succeeds in finding a foothold will have taken advantage of the death of an already established adult. The wastage is so great that no more than one out of several million larvae ever survives to maturity.

The drawbacks of the constant competition and the overcrowding of the teeming populations are evident; what are not so readily seen are the beneficial results of crowding. Sea birds that nest in colonies—for example, the gannets—have a higher rate of reproduction in proportion to the size and density of the colonies; indeed, sometimes in very small colonies no young are produced at all. The whole question of the value to sea birds of dense colonies has been much in dispute among ornithologists; but it does appear that the larger the colony, the greater the visual and auditory stimulation to breeding. There is little dispute, at any rate, about the biological benefits of crowding in an oyster bed. The oysters in a tidal estuary grow in the same place year after year, new generations attaching themselves atop the shells of their parents; in this way, the oysters are kept above the increasing deposits of mud that would otherwise suffocate them. At first glance, it likewise might appear that a group of the spiny shore animals known as sea urchins would compete with each other less if they were spread farther apart. Yet they are often found crowded under the fronds of kelp or Irish moss. The biological benefit of such crowding is that it keeps off predators with a more formidable array of spines than one or even a few sea urchins could muster; and the young sea urchins, with their spines still little developed, gain protection from the presence of the better-armored adults.

Among the crowded inhabitants of the shore, it is inevitable that strange partnerships and accommodations for living should have developed. Two or more different species may live side by side without any serious harm to any and with benefits at least to one. Such an association is known as "commensalism"—literally, "eating from the same table," although the partnership may involve benefits in shelter, transportation, or a place for attachment, as well as in obtaining food. Full-grown horseshoe crabs found on the northeastern coast often have various species of mollusks, barnacles, and even tubeworms attached to the top of their shells. The horseshoe crab is not seriously harmed by these other animals, although probably they do slow it down somewhat; however, this is possibly balanced by the camouflage they afford the crab. The real benefit, however, is to the animals that have found a place of attachment not available on the crowded rocks.

Sometimes the partnership between species produces benefits for all, and is then known as mutualism. A classic example is the relation between the hermit crab, a small worm, and a sea anemone. The hermit crab's long abdomen is only thinly protected, but it has evolved the behavioral mechanism of seeking out the empty shells of snails and carrying them about, with only its legs and head protruding. These snail shells may also shelter small worms. When the crab inserts its long abdomen into the snail shell, the worm then enters a mutual partnership with the crab; it keeps the inside of the shell clean and, in return, snatches particles of the food the crab collects. Sometimes the snail shell inhabited by a hermit crab may also carry a sea anemone placed on top by the crab itself. The anemone benefits by being transported to fresh feeding grounds, and the crab has the benefit of the camouflage offered by the anemone and also of the protection against predatory fish of the anemone's stinging cells.

The shore is a place of constant change, where tides change as the moon waxes and wanes, where the level of land and sea rises and falls, where the waves claim portions of the land; and change, whether gradual or sudden, is met by patterns of life along the shore. When the stages of change in groups of living things are fairly orderly and predictable, scientists call them "succession." They can be observed on a mudflat that has been swept clean of surface life by a storm. The mud may first be colonized by oysters; if competition is absent, they will soon carpet the surface of the mud. The oysters will then have transformed an unstable mud bottom into a substratum not unlike solid rock, so that it becomes a favorable habitat for mussels. As the mussels increase in numbers, the oysters are gradually smothered. Thus, the second stage in the succession is the total replacement of the oysters by a thriving colony of mussels growing on top of their shells. Later, barnacles may become attached to the shells of the mussels in sufficient numbers to kill them. But this third stage is usually short-lived: after the death of the mussels, their shells break loose and the waves carry away the mussel shells along with the barnacles. The chances are that river and ocean currents will deposit a new layer of mud on top of the old oyster bed, and that the sequence

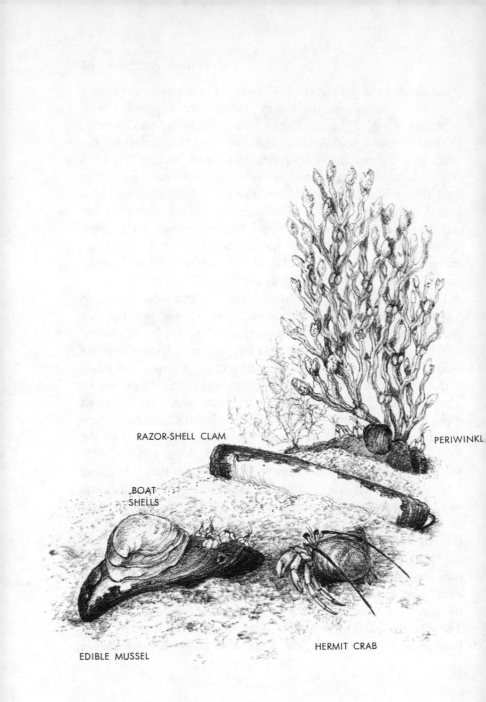

RAZOR-SHELL CLAM

PERIWINKL

BOAT
SHELLS

EDIBLE MUSSEL

HERMIT CRAB

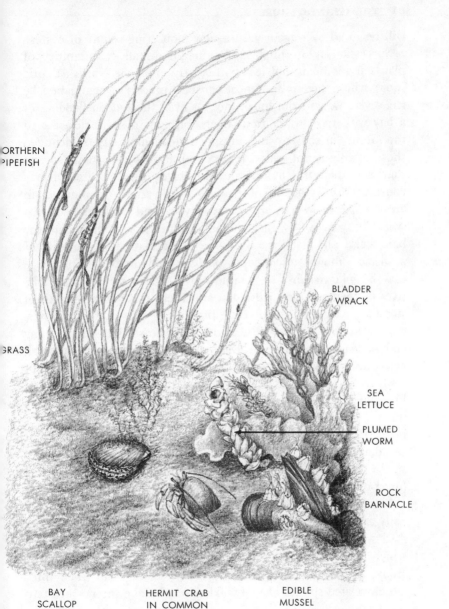

NORTHERN
PIPEFISH

BLADDER
WRACK

GRASS

SEA
LETTUCE

PLUMED
WORM

ROCK
BARNACLE

BAY
SCALLOP

HERMIT CRAB
IN COMMON
PERIWINKLE SHELL

EDIBLE
MUSSEL

will begin all over again with a new pioneering colony of oysters.

Succession is an important principle in all communities of plants and animals; but it is particularly so on the North Atlantic shore, where there is an almost constant process of denudation by ice, severe waves from hurricanes, or even the sudden flooding of a bay with fresh water from rivers, bringing a sharp decrease in the salinity of the bay and causing sudden mortality. A denuded shore usually is not suited to recolonization by the same species that were there just before, and the stages of recolonization may continue over a period of perhaps four years. For example, in areas where rockweeds are crushed by ice and boulders and then swept away by waves, these plants cannot at once repopulate the bare rocks. The first stage would be the formation on the rocks of a surface film of microscopic bacteria and diatoms. This stage may be followed first by a rapid growth of hydroids (small relatives of anemones and jellyfish), and then by a feltlike growth of small algae. It is the small algae that finally offer shelter to a new growth of young rockweeds; as the rockweeds take hold, growing and increasing in numbers, they eventually crowd out the small algae, until the state of the rock is the same as before the ice swept it clear. Sometimes, however, the orderly sequence is interrupted by a physical change in the environment or by the action of some other living thing at the shore. The red algae that abound on rocks in the tidal zone would be expected to coat them completely; but this does not happen in places where large numbers of limpets and snails browse on the algae, maintaining open glades amid the forest of seaweeds.

Most scientists believe that life originated in the seas and gradually crossed over from a marine environment to one on dry land. And some scientists believe that the evolutionary stages through which life passes in the transition to dry land can still be seen by studying the animals and plants at the shore today. The three closely-related species of periwinkles found along the northeastern coast may possibly illustrate just such a sequence of steps from the sea to land; none of the periwinkles is now wholly marine, nor has any of the three yet completed its passage to a life independent of the sea. The obtuse periwinkle, with its large rounded shell, is still closely tied to the sea. As the tides retreat, it seeks out the moisture it needs under the dripping fronds of rockweed. Even its spawning is keyed to the perpetual moisture found in this zone. Rather than shedding its eggs directly into the sea, whence they might be carried by the currents to some place too dry for the young, the periwinkle eggs are laid in a gelatinous mass directly on the fronds of the rockweed; there the eggs develop and the young hatch out complete with shells, ready at once to colonize the moist rockweeds, their only sanctuary from desiccation.

The common periwinkle, the largest found on the North Atlantic shore, represents a different stage in the transition from sea to dry land. It inhabits a much wider range of habitats—on bare rock, among the seaweeds or the stones, and even on the sand; it can endure much greater periods of drying out than the smooth periwinkle can, and it is sometimes even found high on the beach, where it is submerged only briefly at high tide. Although the common periwinkle appears already to have traveled most of the road to a life on land, that really is not so: it is still bound to the sea by the fact that it must shed its eggs directly into the water.

Of the three, the rough periwinkle seems the most likely eventually to adopt a land existence. It inhabits the highest zones on the beach, from mid-tide level up to the splash zone, and it has cast off its dependence on the sea for reproduction. The rough periwinkle, like the other two, has a gill for breathing; but this organ is much reduced in size, and the gill cavity is so richly supplied with blood vessels that it apparently can function almost like a lung, taking the oxygen it requires directly from the air. Its bonds to the sea have been severed by the simple fact that the eggs develop inside the female's body, emerging as perfectly formed living young, miniature periwinkles already covered with tiny shells. Of course no one can predict the future course of evolution with certainty, but it is possible that some further mutations in the rough periwinkle will result in a species as little dependent on the sea as the garden snail.

All of these patterns of life at the shore are at once fluid and definite, as are the animals adapted to them, life's formalized energies. Particular needs are associated with particular places— the barnacle on its rock, the tubeworm in its burrow under the sand. Perhaps it is even possible to look at an animal and see in its multitudes of patterns the shore region that is its home, recreating sand grains from a trumpet worm, warm summer water from an oyster, rockweed from the smooth periwinkle, or salt-marsh peat from the marsh snail. Nature may not be quite this definable. Each habit, each adaptation, proves the general diversity; but the rocky shore and the tidepools, the sandy beach and the dunes, the muddy estuary and the salt marsh, each in its own way distinct in whatever part of Canada or New England it may be found, can also be divided into component parts, into the further units of environment and life.

# ABUNDANCE ON ROCKY SHORES

**4**

THE MAINE COAST, with its rocky headlands, stony beaches, rock ledges, and boulders makes not for poverty but fertility. This may be hard to appreciate when you are faced with little more than a gray granite surface and the rolling sea. But the sea is an enormous fertility in itself, and the rock, with all its cracks and crevices, corners, and varying faces, is a place where lives on the sea's periphery can attach themselves. This becomes more obvious when the tide begins to ebb, showing the profuse growth of algae that covers the rock below the high-tide line, in carpets and fringed curtains that hide a multitude. The wet weed is a host to all kinds of life: snails, prickly sea urchins, scurrying little crabs, worms, and periwinkles, jellyfish, and sponges. It crawls with activity. The rock and the innumerable communities it shelters are in direct alliance with tidal rise and fall and the bounty of salt water. The legions of barnacles that cover it have a direct association with the food that is carried by sea currents, washed back and forth along the inshore depths.

On a coast so full of island turnings, coves, and watery stretches, the land itself has an integral bond with the sea whose mists reach miles in from the shore. The marine moisture makes it possible for the usnea lichen or "old man's beard" to grow and hang in long strands, waving and streaming in the wind, from the spruce trees back of the water, attracting, in turn, the little blue parula warbler, which uses this special material for its nest. The spruce woods growing down to the shore have banks of green moss on their floors, and cloud-gray and gray-green lichen flowing with sunlight where it strikes through, making a hoary brightness on the ground; and they hold bits of crab shells, sea urchins, or mussels—the middens of the herring gulls.

In these woods, typical of shores along the many-islanded bays of Maine, such as Muscongus or Casco, one is never far from a sense of the sea. The inlets and the coves ring with the musically guttural cry of gulls and with the waves lapping and swashing in. Bird sounds, the sounds of the sea, and the sea airs, run constantly through the trees. The white-breasted nuthatch, with a boat-rounded body, travels up and down the tree trunks, announcing itself with a buzzy honking. Smaller, red-breasted nuthatches feed over the ground, moving sometimes from tree trunks to litter of needles with little whisking motions, constantly chittering faintly to each other. A hermit thrush peals out of a dark distance. Red squirrels leap and chatter along the branches. There are trim little brown wrens making rapid melodious sounds in these woods, and flycatchers, slate-colored juncos, and warblers at various seasons. Chickadees, with a nearly continuous conversation of their own, are busy the year round; sometimes they chase each other, playfully swinging behind and between the trees. Crows call; ravens croak from the treetops. At night there may be the chewing, grunting, and snuffling of a porcupine, the sharp yapping of a fox in a field beyond the trees, or the hooting of a great-horned owl from some shaggy branch.

Close to shore, you can see the tidal waters swelling and rising between the trunks of the trees. The wind rides through spruce and fir with the swinging latitude of the sea, from which they may be removed by only a few yards; at the same time they constitute unique inland places where birds, insects, or mammals of the forest community are bound together in need and in attention.

The evergreen forests behind the shore are dark, though light often columns in from above in a spectacular way. Comparatively few wildflowers grow under their shade, although wintergreen and bunchberry find it to their liking, and pink lady-slippers bloom out of the spruce needles in the month of June. The trees grow to considerable size a few hundred yards from the sea, but the closer they are the lower and more scraggly their growth, their branches swept by the wind to the inland side like banners. There appears also to be an increasing hazard for trees, as the number of dead and dying ones and their fallen trunks increase close to the shore. Storms belabor them, and occasional hurricanes make wide swaths through such a forest, leaving open slashed areas where white-throated sparrows jump down, tails flicking, to disappear in fallen branches and reappear again in all their alertness.

The composition of the forest also changes as it grows closer to the shore. The balsam fir can live even at the edge of the sea, but the red spruce gradually thin out and are replaced by white spruce. A spruce tree, being shallow-rooted, can cling to a rock

MOCCASIN
FLOWER

WINTERGREEN

and lean over the water with just enough soil for subsistence. Out on the islands, capes, and peninsulas, the long jutting points of land along Maine's coast, spruce is much in evidence, but farther inland the pines, especially the white, are more predominant, along with deciduous trees. The cold waters of the Gulf of Maine, the thin soil, and the biting wind produce harsh seaside conditions which the spruce apparently can endure better than pine or other potential competitors. Red and white spruce and balsam fir are not the only kinds of trees that grow near the borders of salt water, though they give the coast much of its distinctive character. Black spruce is a smaller species, with a slender trunk and short branches, growing well in poorly drained, boggy areas, but scantily on rocky slopes. Hemlock and northern white cedar are found in intermittent stands above the shore, with varying amounts of white and red pines and a few pitch and jack pines.

These forests where spruce is the dominant tree are subject to disastrous fires. Hundreds and even thousands of acres may be returned to a condition approaching primal bare rock, though the process of regeneration begins at once. A severe fire burns not only the trees but also the accumulated mat of organic matter on the forest floor. After the humus burns, the rebirth of the forest must begin on impoverished soil, or even on rock further denuded of its cover by heavy rains. The new forest will contain little spruce or balsam fir, or in fact any evergreen except pitch pine, which is the one northeastern evergreen that can survive fire, sending up new sprouts from stumps and roots. The burned-over spruce forest will not reproduce itself at first, and may never do so at all unless the soil is shallow and stony—the harsh conditions which the spruce can survive better than its competitors. However, hardwoods such as oaks and maples, which may have been scattered through the forest, sprout well. Birch and aspen take hold in profusion, having light seeds which, spread by the wind, quickly sprout in a burned-over forest. As a result, an extensive growth of equal-sized birch and aspen usually indicates a past calamity.

Mount Desert Island in Maine provides a recent example of succession in a spruce forest along the rocky shore. After the fire of 1947, which burned some 10,000 acres within Acadia National Park, the mature spruce and fir forests were gone, along with a great deal of humus that had gradually accumulated on the slopes. The rocky frame of the land, largely pink granite, was laid bare and remains so except where small ground-covering plants and wildflowers, followed by blueberries, took hold after the fire. They were succeeded by a variety of trees that thrive relatively well on thin or burned-over ground: yellow, gray, and canoe birch, pin or fire cherry, poplar, sumac, and sprouts from the stumps of red oak. It will probably be many decades before the spruce and fir overtop this temporary forest, though their seedlings are now much in evidence. Only when the fallen leaves of hardwoods have created topsoil, and the birches have grown old and died, admitting light to the lower levels where spruce and fir grow, will the evergreens grow rapidly enough to stand above the hardwoods and deprive their competitive seedlings of light.

The original stands along the shore, the virgin, savage, nearly unsurmountable forest, exist only in memory or potentiality. Our mental reconstruction of these forests, described by the nineteenth-century historian Francis Parkman as "vast, continuous . . . dim and silent as a cavern," may be inaccurate, too much colored by the romantic recollections of the last century, although Thoreau's on-the-spot description of the Maine woods makes them dark and deep enough. Longfellow wrote of "the forest primeval," and Parkman amplified his idea of an unbroken forest when he described Verrazano surveying "the shadows and gloom of mighty forests" on the New England shore, Maine as "a waste of savage vegetation," the St. Lawrence River as rolling through the "vastness of lonely woodlands." The romantic view of the untenanted

American wilderness should be tempered by the realization that several million Indians lived north of Mexico at the time of the European discovery, that they had been on the continent for well over fifteen thousand years, and that it was their practice to cut and burn woodland areas for purposes of hunting and agriculture.

Practically all northeastern Indians lived in settlements, some large and permanent, others small seasonal camps. Every village, large or small, meant clearing land for shelters and foraging in nearby forests for fuel, food, building materials, and wood for weapons and tools, thus affecting the forests far from their settlements. A large Iroquois village site, for example, called for the clearing of as much as 150 acres of forest. The woods were regularly burned to clear land for agriculture, as a defense against other Indian tribes, and to increase game animals such as deer by encouraging the low growth of browse that appears after a fire. Any small trees that remained or that took root on the denuded land were methodically cut by the Indian women for use as firewood. Settlers of Boston found the site already so cleared of trees by the Indians that to obtain fuel they had to row across to the wooded drumlin islands in the harbor. One resident of Salem wrote in 1630 that "a man may stand on a little hilly place and see divers thousands of acres of ground as good as need be, and not a tree in the same."

The Saco River of southern Maine appears to have been the northern boundary of forest clearings for maize, and the limit of systematic burning to increase game was at Casco Bay, a little farther up the coast. But these are only approximate boundaries. By the time of European settlement, agriculture and burning had spread far northward, even into the Maritime Provinces of Canada. Although disturbance of the shore forests along the rocky coasts was less than in Massachusetts and southward, the Indians did a certain amount of clearing and firing, and inroads into the forest were made by the early cod-fishing fleets, followed by European settlers.

The early settlements in Maine, however, were confined to toe-holds on the coast, along river mouths and inlets; local industry and trade never really began to thrive until the latter half of the eighteenth century, after the French and Indian wars. Agriculture was at a minimum, with the result that not much land was cleared. If, skirting the shore in a boat nowadays, you are startled to see a cow grazing on a narrow rim of grass between spruce woods and shore rock, it may be a reminder that Maine people are used to keeping cows in just such areas not for dairy farms but for their own subsistence. Two hundred years ago there were few fields and little hay stored for winter use in a country that occupied itself primarily with lumbering, shipbuilding, and fishing. Cows were turned out into natural meadows, or such land as had been burned or cleared, to forage for themselves.

In these shore forests there is often a sharp transition between trees and tides, with only lichen-spotted rocks between. On the borders of inlets, however, or at the head of a cove, a small stony beach with grayish mud may be revealed at low tide, where clam-diggers rake for soft-shell clams. Above that, in a narrow marshy zone between spruce forest and high-tide line, there is likely to be a border of red maple, speckled alder, smooth-leaved viburnum, spirea, wild rose, and blackberries, as well as gray birch and mountain ash; and these merge with a little salt-meadow belt, reached by high tides, of marsh aster, seaside goldenrod, orach, saltwort, and a sparse growth of marsh grasses.

The rocky ledges above tidemark, sloping down to a cove or covering one of the small nearby islands, have only a scanty covering of humus, a covering that may be dried and cracked off by the sun where the rock is steepest, or by freezing and thawing, and is exposed to wind and salt spray so that it erodes easily on its fringes. Dwarfed spruce and prostrate juniper, as well as bayberry and huckleberry, hang on to this thin covering, with roots that help it stay in place; polypody fern grows in rock crevices, and bracken may be anywhere.

A balance is held in these sparse areas between building and eroding. The conditions that made soil in the first place are here, affected by lichens whose acid secretions loosen rock particles and the rotting of plant materials that will be added to these particles, and so are the conditions which take the soil away—wind, drought, snow, and rain. It is quite easy to observe what a hard time the humus has in keeping its foothold, especially on the steeper slopes where it breaks off and slides down little by little, held together almost tentatively in some areas by isolated patches or ridges of moss. These are the places, with their peripheral thickets and stunted trees, where the Lincoln sparrow feeds and skulks, its sweet song coming out of unseen cracks and corners.

Standing high on these ledges or perched boulders, you see the blue, swelling waters stretching between one rock-ledged island after another, with banked trees surmounting them, into the unseen distance. Crows fly around them, gulls wheel, and heavy-bodied ravens sail over the treetops, croaking deeply. Great blue herons feed along the shore at low tide; one of them, when startled, may fly up with a deep "Wark!" to stand in a spruce, the smoky gray-blue plumage fitting the green needles like the blue mists that invest them from the sea. The rolling sea bears in and its surfaces shift to all horizons, and over the sea islands are mottled cloud islands, shifting and regrouping.

A few yards down from juniper and moss and occasional briar thickets merging with bare gray ledge rock, the tidal wash shows its effect, at first in isolated tidepools where the rock has pockets or relatively level spaces, then in companies of small snails and, lower down, of barnacles and fringes of golden rockweed, skirts swinging rhythmically in the waters, below which giant arms of kelp may be swaying. The tidepools are colorful with algae, flicking with small lives. The barnacles in their small, white, calcareous domes are spread everywhere. The rockweed is lush. You go from dominance of rock, the weight of drowned hills, geologic distance manifested, to another kind of monumentality, in which a major theme is that of numbers.

The general observer cannot help being impressed by the things he will never be able to count. A jar or glass of sea water in summer or early fall will be loaded with the white shed skins of barnacles, with feathery fronds—the "feet" or feeding appendages by which they wave food into their shells—showing in detail, along with the spinning, floating, darting creatures of the planktonic world. Crevices in the rock are filled, sometimes several feet deep, with many generations of barnacle shells. Below these may be further depths of shell which have been worn or ground to bits, forming a grayish-white, soft substance. There are acres of blue-black mussels, miles of wandering periwinkles or dog whelks. They come by the shovelful or the truckload, and they suggest a time-honored might in numbers. There are stationary feeders here, wanderers, crawlers, and swimmers, olive-green crustaceans that slip frantically away when disturbed, top-heavy snails with shells rolling over weeds like galleons in a swell, crabs scuttling, and worms wriggling in the mud. The numbers, the life met with over and under and beside every single rock or stone, become a fantasy hardly to be grasped; more than accumulations precisely adapted, they are a sign of the unknown scope of the universe.

The small animals of the rocky shore have distinctive actions, special ways in which they are fitted to varying conditions. The rocky shore is not an easy place in which to live or to maintain a position. In various degrees the intertidal organisms have to survive drying out between tides; they are subject to the action of ice in the winter, to the summer's sun, the rain, the violent surf. They have to exist in air and water in the many conditions between ocean depths and land above the tides. To be dry or wet, wholly or in part, is the condition each of them requires—a condition fulfilled by the waves and the tides.

The zones, the levels these plants and animals have taken for themselves, are suggestive of zones and levels of altitude on land. To trace their counterpart on land would require an arduous ascent from sea level to mountain top. But what makes the gradations of the shore unique is the meeting of land and water. Even in a location where there is virtually no tide, and where the shore is completely protected from wave action, there will still be a narrow zonation of living conditions, and consequently of the organisms themselves.

Scientists have written at length of these intricate and abundant populations of the rocky shore. Zonations are a convenient way of beginning to study these populations, but anyone who lifts the heavy accumulation of rockweed and looks underneath will have a glimpse of their many divisions and interrelations, their many ways of holding on, their many peculiarities honored by ages of living with the sea. There are filter feeders, like mussels, that hang onto rock securely with their byssus threads; there are those which feed on algae, like the periwinkles, and that wander through a restricted range; there are the barnacles, free in their larval stage to float and drift in the open waters, to be dispersed far and wide, and then as adults housed permanently in one place. Limpets also hang onto the rock as with suction cups, but unlike the barnacles they graze, feeding on films of algae or planktonic diatoms that settle on rock surfaces, going out on excursions and returning again to the places they started from.

Very often, when you lift up the curtain of weed, dog whelks will fall off. These are predators, occupying the same general area as common periwinkles, between the middle to lower tide levels. They feed sometimes on periwinkles, but their chief prey are the stationary barnacles and mussels, whose shells they pierce by means of a radula, a toothed ribbon that can be extended at the end of a proboscis. The dog whelks are colorful. They are banded with orange and white or with white and purple, or they may be all white, all yellow, lavender, or brownish-black. The shell's color and shape seem to be an effect of diet, although relative exposure to waves may contribute as well. An increase in the amount of mussels eaten may result in a shell with greater thickening at the lip and more variations in its spiral pattern, but the greatest variations are in color. The pigments in the shells and tissues of mussels are passed on to a whelk that feeds upon them, and it lays down these pigments in its own, usually dark-colored, growing shell; barnacle-fed whelks, on the other hand, are usually white. It also appears that the yellow in the shell is prevalent in areas where whelks are exposed to medium surf, and that here diet is not a factor. Since dog whelks are easily dislodged, they are not usually found on rocks that overhang deep water. In shallower areas their eggs are laid one at a time on rock surfaces, under protective rockweeds, and can often be found there in upright rows of tough little straw-colored capsules. Most of the hundreds of eggs contained in each of these cases are not fertile but serve as food for the few whelks that will emerge in four months as tiny but fully shelled animals.

Many ways have been devised to grade intertidal plants and animals, but the simplest is to divide their realm into three zones. Seaward from the interior that is wholly land is a belt reached only by extreme high tides, called the Littorina Zone after the scientific name of the periwinkles, its clearest indicators. This highest zone has also been called the "black zone" because of the visibly dark band on the rocks showing the presence of blue-green algae, a slippery, thin growth of plants beyond the reach of most tides but splashed by the waves. Here, in crevices where it is relatively secure from the force of the waves, is the rough periwinkle.

The lower limit of the Littorina Zone also sets an upper limit, in terms of true abundance, for the rock or acorn barnacles whose scientific name has been given to the next lower zone, the Balanoid. Some barnacles do, of course, subsist in the Littorina Zone; but it is in the Balanoid that they become really abundant, coating the rocks with their sharp, grayish-white cones. Because of the various kinds of algae associated with these barnacles, the rocks they inhabit have a yellowish-brown cast when seen from a distance. This "yellow" zone ends virtually at low tide, a fringe area where the barnacles cease to be abundant and where they are largely replaced by several kinds of algae and mussels. The Balanoid Zone usually extends from nearly high to nearly low tide levels; and whereas the Littorina Zone is more exposed to the air, this realm of the barnacles is subject to the force of waves and surf, which can vary a great deal with the character of the rocks along the shore—the direction they face, the amount of offshore protection they have, and their degree of steepness.

Some kinds of barnacles have managed to penetrate the high splash zone where the periwinkles live; here they net their food during the few days each month when the sea reaches them, closing their shells tightly in the meantime, to retain the essential moisture inside. But most barnacles are conspicuous inhabitants of the high-tide surf zone—where even the seaweeds, so tugged and hauled and battered, manage to survive only in a stunted form—and in this zone their only real competitors are mussels.

Barnacle shells cover rocks like the indefinite buildings of some miniature metropolis, under the washing of the sea; but the animal that constructs them is usually easier to observe in a relatively protected area. At low tide, all you see is a limy, conelike shell of six plates, but when the sea water comes up again and covers it, two tight valves in the center of this miniature volcano open up, and a momentary shadow appears to flicker over it, disappearing as suddenly as it came. Rhythmically, the valves open, and a plumelike feeding appendage waves back and forth, acting as a net to pull in diatoms and other microscopic plants and animals from the sea water.

The animal inside the barnacle shell has none of the characteristics of a mollusk—a snail, clam, or oyster—but is similar to a shrimp. When its valves are open it is in effect standing on its head and waving its "feet" out into the water. The only sedentary member of the group known as the crustaceans, it is a relative of

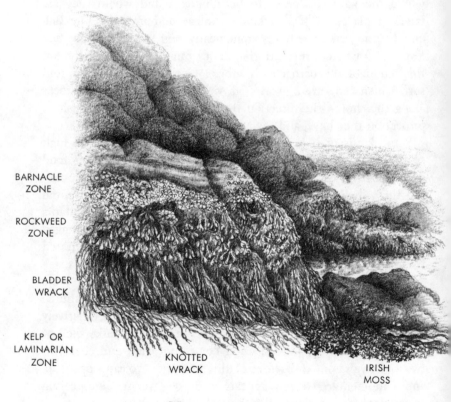

BARNACLE ZONE

ROCKWEED ZONE

BLADDER WRACK

KELP OR LAMINARIAN ZONE

KNOTTED WRACK

IRISH MOSS

**Marine Algae Zonation**

lobsters, shrimp, crabs, and beachfleas. When hatched, young barnacles pass their first larval stage as tiny creatures with one eye, three pairs of legs and a minute one-valve shell, after which they molt and turn into larvae with two eyes, six pairs of legs and a bivalve shell, all in a period of about three months. In its second stage the barnacle larva abandons its floating life and moves shoreward, avoiding light and responding positively to gravity, so that it descends from sea surfaces to rock. There it may spend an hour or so moving over the rock surface, seemingly testing it with legs and antennae, before choosing where to settle down. It may even abandon such a rock completely and drift with the tide again, to try other regions. A barnacle larva's final selection may have something to do with the relative roughness of the rock surface, but it is probably influenced more by the chemical "scent" released into the water by adult barnacles. This may largely explain why the rock-cemented cones of barnacles are so densely concentrated.

In the final stage of this curious development, the young barnacle attaches itself headfirst by suckerlike antennae to the solid base on which it will spend the rest of its life. Then it begins to secrete the cement which will form its protective shell, while its tissues undergo reorganization into an adult without legs or eyes; within half a day the little animal has imprisoned itself in its cone-shaped apartment. A barnacle that survives the attacks of predators, grinding ice, and tumultuous surf may live for as long as three years. After its death the shell remains attached to the rock, and new generations of barnacles eventually cover it; meanwhile, the empty shell may also serve as a refuge for other forms of life attempting to gain a foothold on the crowded shore, such as the young of periwinkles, tubeworms, or anemones.

The third and lowest region of the shore is uncovered only by the lowest tides; it is called the Laminarian Zone, after its brown algae or kelps, the Laminaria. Unlike algae growing higher on the shore, the long, elastic fronds of the Laminaria are so constructed as to withstand the constant surging and drawing back of the water; they have great tensile strength, and their environment does not subject them to the intense light to which the weeds of higher zones are exposed for several hours a day. In this "brown" zone the large and long members of the kelp family swing back and forth with the movement of the sea. One of the most typical of these kelps is the horsetail, whose single, broad, flat frond is cut into ribbons and offers a minimum resistance to the water. If the horsetail is pulled up, by a firm grip on the stalk, most of its holdfast is likely to come with it; also, its branches may reveal a representative cross section of the animal life of this zone. Blue mussels are usually attached to the upper surface of the holdfast, with an occasional horse mussel, a visitor from farther offshore. The horse mussel is held in place against the force of the waves by a dense tangle of threads spun from a milky secretion that hardens upon contact with sea water, just as the spider's silk hardens when exposed to the air. These threads often act as a sieve, catching pebbles and silt that build up in time as a thick layer of debris, protected by the mussel's large shell and the holdfast of the kelp. The little mud pocket thus produced becomes a nursery for young sea urchins and small worms, and the fragile, thin bodies of brittle stars may also be found there. Among the larger animals that may be brought up out of water on the horsetail kelp are anemones, crumb-of-bread sponges, and rockborer clams which belie their name when they find the New England rocks too tough and bore into the kelp's holdfast instead.

Whether a shore is protected by islands or peninsulas or exposed to the open ocean, it will be characterized by the same three zones of life, although each will have a different proportion of plants and animals. The long, slender knotted wrack, for example, is the conspicuous form on a protected shore. The algae that predominate on the less exposed middle and lower shores below

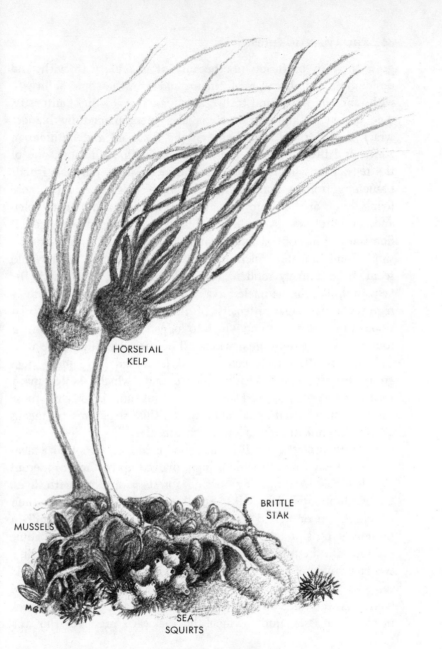

HORSETAIL
KELP

BRITTLE
STAR

MUSSELS

MGN

SEA
SQUIRTS

**Life in Kelp Holdfast**

grow there in profusion not because of an ability to withstand desiccation, but because of their rapid growth, their ability to withstand the waves and to live in a region of low light intensity. The dominant knotted wrack is also accompanied by bladder wrack in the fringe areas between the Balanoid and Laminarian zones, and they are often found growing with Irish moss, one of the red algae, which can be recognized by short purplish fronds branching from a main stem. The Irish moss is one of those living things at the shore that has precise needs and a small tolerance of inhospitable conditions; but where its needs are met, it flourishes. It has only a limited ability to withstand drying out; its short fronds are not much affected by the surf, and so it would seem to be a likely resident of the lowest zone, along with the kelp; still, like the barnacle larva, it has its sensitivities. Irish moss requires a particular intensity of illumination and a particular slope of the substratum on which to lodge, with the result that it is found only in certain areas where all of these conditions are met. Where this attractively colored and fashioned little plant does grow, it is luxuriant, forming dense mats which shelter many forms of life such as starfishes, sea urchins, and bryozoans, those minute animals that build delicate mosslike structures by means of their innumerable interconnected capsules.

With their elastic-tough fronds, the bladder and knotted wracks sway profusely when the tide is high, buoyed up by their numerous air-filled bladders, forming marine forests swarming with lives. Crabs climb up their stalks. Small sea snails creep along their fronds. Clam or nereid worms, their quantities of "gill feet" in motion, swim through the weed pursued by fishes that have come inshore with the tide. Shrimp flutter and dart through the weaving, swaying tangle of fronds and branches, hunting animals of plankton size, tiny larvae, and crustaceans, as well as small fishes and worms. As the tide ebbs, the fronds sag down and lie over the rock in sodden masses, under which the rockweed preserves the wetness of the retreating sea, and life continues. The mussels have pulled in their siphon tubes and closed their shells tightly; but they are a likely prey for starfish, which clasp their shells and inexorably pull them apart by the suction of the tube feet on the underside of their arms. Crabs too, particularly the flat, reddish Jonah crab, continue to scuttle about in search of clams. Now the hunting birds, herring gulls, ravens, and crows, aware of the opportunity which low tide gives them to forage in the exposed rockweed, begin to poke around for periwinkles, mussels, and crabs.

In this teeming world of the rocky shore, tidally oriented, constantly in motion, living things are incessantly being transmuted into the food of others, and at the same time it is their function to escape. Organisms contribute to the motion of their environment, the sum of a remorseless energy, not only by eating and being eaten but by provisions for a temporary survival. One of the curious adaptations used in the face of danger is seen in crabs and starfish. These scavengers and predators are themselves subject to being eaten, or to being pinioned or damaged by a stone flung at them by waves. In the face of that possibility they are endowed with a defensive mechanism, the ability to sacrifice a part of their bodies, a claw or an arm, so that the entire animal may survive. This sacrifice and the ensuing regeneration occur in all true crabs, in hermit crabs, and in lobsters. With crabs, as distinct from starfish, a limb does not break off and grow back again at any random place but can be sacrificed at a predetermined point of weakness, specifically an encircling groove on the third segment of the limb, counting from the body. Where it breaks off, the small exposed area is quickly covered by a thin membrane. This stump gradually turns black, but then the new limb begins to regenerate. With each molt and the consequent growth of a larger shell, the stump increases in size, until it catches up with its corresponding member on the other side. This is so common an occurrence that of several crabs caught along the shore at least one is likely to have a limb in the process of regeneration.

Starfishes and brittle stars have the same ability to lose an arm and then regrow it, but there is no specific point where the break must occur, although it often happens where the arm meets the central disk. The name of the brittle star, in fact, refers to the extreme readiness with which this species does lose its limbs. As though this adaptation had gone too playfully and too far, even gentle handling causes a brittle star to lose at least one arm. The starfishes, quite unlike the crabs, do not have to wait for a molt in order to have a lost arm regenerated, but begin almost immediately to send out a budlike growth from the stump. Provided there is enough left of the body region to which it is attached, only one arm or ray may be reconstituted into a whole new starfish— hence the futility of trying to get rid of starfish preying on oyster and clam beds by hacking them to bits.

Along the rocky shore are countless numbers of starfishes: young ones less than half an inch in diameter found under meadows of Irish moss; or such species as the northern starfish, found in the lower, ebb-tidepools; or the blood-red starfish, a deep-water animal that may be found in the lowest zones. Like many other marine animals, the starfish looks remarkably simple, or at least so remote from more familiar organisms that we imagine it to be so. In fact, it is an extremely complex animal despite the complete lack of an excretory system, a primitive respiration system, and no organs of circulation at all as we commonly use the term. Perhaps the complexity appears less surprising in light of modern biology which places animals with backbones, including man, in an evolutionary line of descent from these same starfishes and their relatives the sea urchins, sand dollars, and sea cucumbers. By any standard the nervous system of the starfish is elaborate. Its equipment also includes the unusual hydraulic-pressure mechanism by which it moves its many pairs of tube feet, and which enables it to

Jonah Crab at Edge of Tidepool

hold on so hard to a rock that a hundred pounds of pressure may be required to pull it off.

In addition, the starfish has a remarkable and unique feeding mechanism, which had mystified naturalists since Aristotle until it was recently explained. Seen from above, the starfish appears merely to glide over the surface of its prey—a clam, oyster, or mussel—draping its arms about it, and remaining there as though asleep for several hours. But when it has finally moved off, the two shells of the bivalve can be opened easily, and its contents will have been devoured. At one time it was thought that the starfish was able to inject a poison between the valves to kill the clam and cause the shell to open. Another theory, now known to be the correct one, is that the starfish has strength enough to pry the shells apart. In fact, the suction exerted by a starfish's tube feet is equal to the twelve or more pounds of force required to open the shell of an ordinary clam. It has also been discovered, however, that the shell does not have to be opened very far. An aperture of a twenty-fifth of an inch is enough to permit a starfish to work its large stomach, turned inside out, between the two halves of the shell. In feeding it is aided by an enzyme so powerful that it can digest living tissue even after being diluted by sea water.

Species of animals from offshore depths may also visit the swaying zone of the kelp, just as marine fish from deeper water swim closer inshore on the flood of the tide. One of these, the great red jellyfish, with a huge disk and deadly tentacles up to fifty feet long, is swept at times during early autumn into coves and bays from its native habitat in the open sea. For some jellyfishes the sequence in the reproductive cycle is tied to the rocky shore. White jellyfish, for example, are often swept shoreward during the summer. By fall, all of the adults of this species have died, but they leave their young behind them in the form of tiny plantlike creatures attached to rock in the Laminarian Zone. All summer, the common moon jellyfishes are carried in by tides that leave their crumpled, glittering bodies strewn along the shore. Their water-filled corpses evaporating in the sun are often cursed by local bathers, who might regard them with less dismay if they knew that this represented the final step in the moon jelly's elaborate life cycle. Earlier in the summer, groups of moon jellies in great numbers drift offshore, speckling the sea. At this time the adults carry larval jellyfish which must somehow reach the shore in order to develop further —and they provide for this with the mechanism of their own death. These moon jellies, which have ceased all resistance to tides and currents, now drift in over the kelps and the Irish moss and the sharp cones of barnacles; they die in the process, but as a result the larvae are shaken loose. Each larva, which before this had been clinging to lobes below its parent's mouth, now glides away and attaches itself to the bottom. In the form of a polyp only about an eighth of an inch long, the larva spends the winter near the low-tide line. In late winter or early spring it begins to change shape: it grows longer, divides into a series of discs, like a miniature stack of saucers, each of which is detached to swim away, a complete though still tiny jellyfish.

In the mutuality of rock and water, land and sea, no area is more intriguing and various than the tidepool or rockpool. No one of these pools is like another. Any one may be more or less associated with the Littorina, Balanoid or Laminarian zone, but each has its special conditions, a balanced population of its own. From the highest level to the lowest, where these rock-walled pools are out of contact with sea water only at extreme low tide, there are as many variations as there are communities for which salt water provides the one uniform condition. A pool high up on the splash zone may be filled only occasionally, and contain never more than a few inches of salt water; it must be replenished by rain water if life in it is to exist. Dip your fingers into one of these pools on a sunny day in the springtime, even when offshore waters are very cold, and you will find it almost lukewarm, although during the night the temperature may have dropped to thirty or forty degrees. Such extremes make a high rockpool a difficult environment for life, and the hazards are increased by a great variation in the production of carbon dioxide and oxygen during the day and night. During the day, for example, the water is usually saturated with oxygen, visible as rising bubbles, because of the photosynthetic activity of algae. At night, both the algae and the animals of the pool give off carbon dioxide, and the oxygen content may fall below the minimum requirements for certain animals.

The constant changes in temperature, salinity, oxygen, and carbon dioxide, the alternating dryness and wetness, characterize a world in which animals and plants left behind by tidal waters must adjust to an especially exacting environment. The warm sun bakes rock slopes above the sea and they steam after the cold surf washes them and withdraws, pouring through cracks and crevices. There are hours at low tide when tidepools hardly move; when the tide rises again, and sways and stirs their plumose world, they are replenished by the water which is life. There are spiral-like blond and green clumps of algae reaching up through shallow water, soft, light-green sea lettuce, patches of light-rose algae, and others reddish-brown and deep green, orange and ocher, and where the water is deepest there are roofs of writhing, swinging golden rockweed.

Even when the surf is at its most turbulent, pounding, inrushing, trickling, and splashing, these gardens keep a swaying stability. Tiny fish often dart here and there, or stand suspended in the shadows. An olive-colored crustacean climbs or hops erratically out of a pool onto sun-warmed rock for a few seconds and then returns, to swim like a fish. The working, feathery foot of a barnacle makes a shadow play on sun-shimmered, underwater rock. Blue mussels and horse mussels cling to the rocky walls or are wedged in crevices, and there are starfishes that feed on them.

Spiny sea urchins graze on algae; rockpool shrimps, nearly transparent, dart backward in the water; and a little closer investigation with a hand lens, or of a sample under a microscope, can disclose an unsuspected realm, closely inhabited, stirring and delicate.

Some of the animals that live in rockpools are obliged to endure particular exactitudes and changes while being more or less fixed in place; others, though native to that environment, are able to wander a little. *Anurida maritima*, for example, is a tiny creature of gunmetal hue, one of the few saltwater insects, which often moves from upper level pools closer to shore to scavenge for food. Its body is covered with a coating of hair or bristle that retains a bubble of air and enables it to breathe under water, surviving changes in the tide. It is able to walk on the surface film of water without any trouble, though it is not a swimmer. Most of the time, *Anurida* is seen not as an individual but as part of a mass—little dark blue-gray patches drifting on the water surface, or sometimes only a few together curling and uncurling like minute leaves. This is an apparent helplessness. Almost any breeze across the water surface makes them slide together like people slipping on the ice. They skip off rocks, meet, and flick apart through moist crevices; they are swept by wind across a pool; yet in an almost magnetic way they tend to keep together, or rejoin sooner or later. Perhaps this is what the ecologist W. C. Allee called "contagious distribution" in animals. As you observe them, you think not so much of their helplessness on the water as of their communal behavior, their dispersal, and at the same time their affinity, the race of *Anurida* in action. This action is not separate from the ripples and mercurial motions of the water surface; it is a paradigm of restlessness.

The opposite of the *Anurida* and their erratic motion is an animal so totally immobile that it appears no less a plant than any of the algae in a pool. The crumb-of-bread sponge spreads like a shapeless, light-green film over the rocks that are exposed to the sea, sometimes covering the entire bottom of a pool like a mat. When it grows elsewhere, in quieter waters away from the surf zone, this sponge is not forced to lose all shape and to become streamlined against the waters, but instead forms a miniature moonscape of volcanolike green cones. Its color is the green of the chlorophyll-bearing algae that live in its tissues. The crumb-of-bread sponge does not have the apparent structure of a bath sponge, but its shapelessness reveals it to be a native of the restless shore rather than of the quiet depths of the ocean bottom. Formless though it may appear, the crumb-of-bread does have a framework made up of spicules—transparent, double-pointed needles of silica, which for all their lightness have the strength of a tubular scaffolding.

A rockpool floor is paved with colors and forms. The limy-pink coralline algae are very conspicuous there; they are able to make carbonate of lime a part of their tissues and so convert a limp seaweed into a hard crust. A careful observer sees the feathery tracings of hydroids, and looks into the strange realm of the marbled, pink, or rich-brown anemones. Man in his whimsy has named sea animals after completely dissimilar animals of the land—sea horses, sea hares, sea lions; but perhaps he has come a degree closer, with respect to color and texture, in naming the sea lettuce, an alga of the shore, after a garden vegetable. The marine anemone is an animal named after no animal at all, but after a woodland plant, also called the windflower. Its only resemblance to the windflower lies in its inclination to evade the wind—another paradox in nomenclature—and, in its symmetry, as perfect as a flower.

Sea anemones are found in the lowest levels of the tidal zone, but they can be seen best in rockpools where shallow water remains between the tides. Here, when the tide falls, the anemone pulls its wavy tentacles into the column of its body which then flattens. But in a rockpool still filled with water after ebb tide, the huddled masses of anemone, nearly touching, continue to feed, and their crowns of flowerlike tentacles may be seen in action. Their beauty is also a menace. A plumose anemone may have a thousand tentacles, giving it the look of a showy chrysanthemum; and each of these tentacles bears several thousand tiny stinging cells, darts that shoot out on contact with the animal's prey, to entangle it and finish it off with poison.

The populace of the tidepools varies from level to level, and from pool to pool. High on the shore one of these natural aquariums, severely exposed to sun and air, may have only a few species of plants and animals—possibly the green tube-seaweeds known as Enteromorpha, some clusters of *Anurida maritima*, a few browsing periwinkles, and some barnacles. Farther down, life becomes more prodigal, and in the colorful pools closest to the shore rarer species may be found—cold-water coral, rockpool shrimp, barnacle larvae, sea slugs, and sea urchins.

In the rocking seas, offshore bell buoys may be clanging, and among the islands and peninsulas the waters are lined with buoys that mark the underwater traps of lobstermen. In the larger bays there are confusing turns, changes of mood from one corner to another, vistas wide and narrow, through fogs and mists, constantly new tricks of light and air. The sea always seems to spread and shift from one distance to the next, dangerous and enticing. The lobster boats drone and putter through the early morning mists, the sea-wet air. The lobstermen guide them with skill alongside their markers, swinging by, slowing up, stopping but letting their engines idle—almost in a single motion—while they pull up their basketlike traps to investigate the contents. They throw a few undersized lobsters overboard, plug the claws of others which they throw into the boat, rebait the trap, and move on while throwing the trap back into the water, with no waste effort.

Lobsters off Maine, incidentally, were not always so small as they are likely to be today, if we can rely on the journal entry of

Captain George Weymouth in 1605: "And towards night we drew with a small net of twenty fathoms very nigh the shore; we got about thirty very good and great lobsters." The great lobsters have long since disappeared, for too many are taken, and the small size-limit allows them to be caught too soon. As early as 1823 it was necessary to pass laws to control the Maine lobster fishery, and in this century many of the lobsters come from hatcheries or man-tended beds. It is rare in Maine to see one of the really large lobsters outside of an aquarium. A lobster allowed to attain its full size may weigh thirty pounds, two-thirds of it in the enormous claws.

Across the water, black double-crested cormorants travel back and forth, bodies stretched straight out, like dark pine knots with wings. They dive from the surface of the water when fishing, dipping over and into it quickly and quietly, and after feeding they stand on island rocks with their ragged wings stretched out to dry in the sun. Sanderlings with twinkling legs feed in the shallows, and spotted sandpipers teeter along the shore. During the nesting season an osprey may fly on a regular route between the islands with a fish in its talons. Black guillemots suddenly fly off low over the water before an oncoming boat like so many great black and white butterflies. Or a black duck spins up as it takes wing. Traveling by outboard, you may see harbor seals lying like sacks over rocky shoals, or a head with large brown eyes may bob up next to the boat and then disappear, an embodiment of curiosity. Then a loon, whose haunting, quavering cry is an inviolable part of the wilderness, back of human history, heard when the loud noise of the shaking motor stops at last and you drift on the waters, conscious of how much they sweep and the winds sweep, and of how much control and experience, how much saltwater knowledge through wind and fog and wave is needed to be even relatively confident on the sea.

Rain follows mist and intermittent sunlight, pouring straight down through the spruce, trickling from its waxy needles. Nearby islands are dark and gray, seen only dimly. Across the coves and inlets big round drops fall on the long flat surfaces so that they skip and dance, the plays and essays of water and air fanned or flayed out in reaches of gray and silver. An unseen lobster boat hums ponderously. Waves slap and chuck in along the shore, the rocky shore with its numberless beings and associations.

# THE REALM OF SAND

**5**

INSTEAD OF THE ANGULAR CHARACTER of boulder and ledge, instead of the dark, pinnacled spruce and the rockweeds swinging in the tides, the sandy shores are for the most part low lying and flat, though they have their cliffs and banks, with sunlight and wind catching everywhere on leaves, beach grass, and grains of sand. "Oke is the chief wood," declared Captain John Smith when he made a landfall in southern New England in 1615, and his statement is equally true today. Its deep green color is the prevailing sight from northern Massachusetts southward. Oak farther inland may alternate with other species of deciduous trees, or with white pine and with pockets or woods of pitch pine. The oaks thin out above the sea, to survive as woods of dwarf trees where there are sheltered and relatively moist hollows. Their annual new growth is continually being killed by salt spray, and the result of this pruning back is a low, rounded copse, like the top of a close-cropped head, fitting neatly into its hollow above the sea. It is a small sand-floored forest, visited by rabbits and by skunks on the prowl for beetles and grubs, as well as songbirds, and it is full of the rattling and shaking of limbs and last year's leaves. Stands of scrub oak, glistening with light, may stretch for miles along a cliff above the sea, no more than a few feet high, though the trees of which they are composed may be of considerable age. These "scrub barrens" were once the home of the now extinct heath hen.

Pitch pines survive in protected pockets behind a beach, also as trees of stunted, shrublike size. These are more susceptible to injury by salt spray than the scrub, or bear, oak. It is possible that when the white settlers first arrived pitch pines were relatively isolated along the coast, although they spread later and now cover a great part of Cape Cod, Nantucket, eastern Long Island, and many other sandy shores between Boston and the Hudson River. Although Long Island had inland pitch pine barrens from the earliest times, Cape Cod's pitch pine forests seem to have spread from plantings, reported by Thoreau in the nineteenth century, when much of the local terrain had been reduced to a very bare and bleak condition. The indigenous hardwoods of New England that touched the shore, including beech, oak, and maple, were laid low at a fairly early date.

Pitch pines used to be exploited for their resin, for making turpentine and axle grease, and as fuel for locomotives, and they were employed in boiling down water to extract salt. They were also once burned for charcoal, in tryworks for whales, and in iron foundries. As late as 1909, about 600,000 board feet annually were used for the manufacture of boxes and crates in Massachusetts alone. As their use for man-made fires reduced the pitch pines, so forest fires explain their survival. The trees grow in open stands that let in plenty of light, and the litter of their dried-out needles, cones, and branches is extremely combustible. However, a fire, except when it is particularly severe, does not destroy the pitch pines, since they are one of the very few conifers that can sprout again from underground roots after their trunks are burned. As forest fires have been prevented during the past twenty or thirty years, oaks have come back to replace the pitch pines in a number of areas, and may eventually dominate them if fires are reduced to a minimum. A pitch pine is an "intolerant" tree, greedy for light, and will die off when overtopped and shaded by an oak.

On the inland side of a sandy beach there are thickets of beach plum and bayberry, interspersed with the *Rosa rugosa* or "salt spray rose," an introduced plant from the Orient that is able to survive an exposure to salt spray which would be fatal to other roses. Hollows and relatively sheltered slopes may be carpeted with clumps of *Hudsonia* or beach heather, a gray-green, many-branched, small-leaved plant that bears bright yellow flowers in the month of June; and between them there may be mats of dry, curly, many-fronded deer moss. Bearberry or hog cranberry is also one of the heath family, a ground cover with small shiny leaves and with red berries in the fall, that covers wide areas along some parts of the shore, growing densely and helping to bind the sandy soil. It is, however, vulnerable to being trampled or driven over. A passing beach buggy will kill the bearberry plants under its wheels and leave brown scars for a long time to come.

The beach pea also grows along the shore and on the upper levels of a beach, often in conjunction with the seaside goldenrod. Above the reach of the waves, and in sandy inland heath areas, sometimes lying in pitch pine barrens, is the broom crowberry, a shrubby, woody evergreen plant with very small leaves like the beach heather, whose isolation is of particular interest to botanists. In a pre-glacial era, apparently, it grew all along the coastal

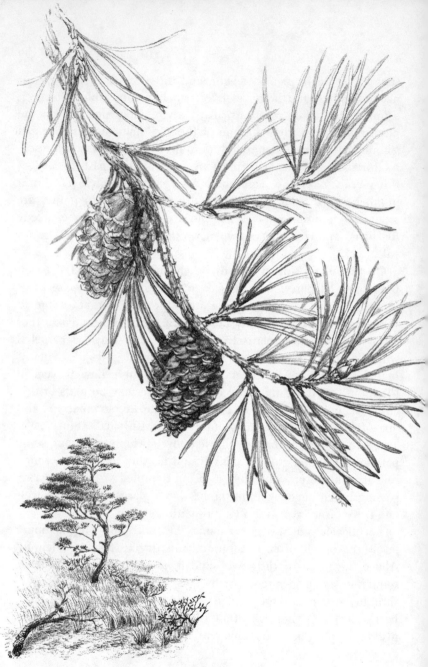

**Pitch Pine**

plain from the Carolinas to Labrador. When the sea level rose after the glaciers receded and the continental shelf was drowned, it survived only in high areas along the coast, so that it can now be found in such widely separated places as the New Jersey pine barrens, Cape Cod, Nantucket, Mount Desert Island, and Newfoundland.

All these plants help in some degree to keep sand from blowing, but the prime stabilizer is beach grass, also called marram grass (from the Latin *mare*, the sea). Its leaf blades—stiff, sharply-pointed, coarse-textured, and at the same time almost satiny—are rolled slightly inward, minimizing water loss by reducing their surface area. When they droop toward the sand they inscribe circles around their stems in the manner of a compass. Beach grass stands throughout the year, straw-yellow in fall and winter, its seed heads curving before the wind against white sands and blue water, strong in its right of holding down the shifting landscape. Its stems rise from long, interconnected systems of rhizomes, ending in fibrous roots that reach for water deep under the sands. Because it grows fast enough to grow along with accumulations of blowing sand without being inundated, this plant can stabilize a "blown out" area, keeping the sand from migrating.

The shore is a rigorous environment, and the plants that are able to subsist there along with the beach grass are adapted to it in very special ways. They maintain themselves on the upper levels of a beach, above the farthest line of wrack left by the tide, in the drifted, blackened rockweed, straw, eelgrass and other litter where sandfleas, robber flies, and scavenging beetles can make a living. Here they have to endure the force of pelting sands, strong winds, glaring sunlight, salt spray, and storm waves. Exposed to fall and winter storms with their roaring surf, no plant could possibly survive. The problem of being uprooted every year is solved by annual plants that cast their seeds upon the water, to be dispersed and regenerated in another season. Such is the sea rocket, whose

BEACH
PLUM

POVERTY
GRASS

MGN

**Dune Plants**

seed-filled capsules are carried by the waves to the upper beach and blown uphill where they lodge among the beach grasses.

Plants adapted to living in a dry environment are xerophytes; in order to thrive, they must not be overexposed to the sun's rays, and also they must retain water. Some, like the yellow-green sea-beach sandwort with shiny fat leaves hugging its stem, are "succulents," whose fleshy stems and leaves with waxy coatings are effective in storing water. Others, like seaside spurge, which grows prostrate on the sand in wheel-like rosettes, have small leaves exposing a minimum surface area to the sun, which spread out over the beach to catch whatever rain may fall. Under constant exposure to salt spray, these plants appear also to have developed a capacity to dilute salt in their leaves. The beach pea folds its leaves on hot and glaring days to reduce evaporation.

This is the realm of sand, the beach and dune environment above high tide, subject to occasional storm waves, but governed, unlike the lower tidal areas, more by the wind than by the waves. By way of definition, it should be pointed out that a beach may also be composed of stones and boulders. In fact, broad and long sandy beaches, with far-reaching flats at low tide, are an important feature of the coastal environment from Massachusetts southward, but they are relatively few along the northeast coast as a whole. Their absence along the coasts of Newfoundland or Maine is explained by the resistant rock, for there has not been time enough for the sea to grind it down and to collect particles into sand. These stony beaches are usually found in pockets at the heads of coves and inlets, or they may be short and narrow, alternating with ledges of rock. Often they are spectacular, covered by enormous and very round boulders in varying shades of gray and green, among which a mink may slip unseen, or an otter pass undetected as it travels to the water in quest of fish.

The great boulders washed by northern seas, or the stones jostled in the surf, are stages along the way from primal rock to

Seaside Goldenrod

grains of sand; or from mountains to mud, since the end result of this erosive process is fine-textured silt. The way is a long one, both in geologic time and in character, from the rocky shores of Maine to the beaches of Martha's Vineyard or Long Island, though each is part of the same process. Sandy beaches may not be as spectacular as the rocky shore. There is a dramatic quality to rock shoulders against the sea, old hills and mountaintops above the tides, the force of earth and the force of water facing each other directly. Still, the sandy beaches have a drama of their own. They are flexible and dynamic. Beach plants, obliged to exist between the extremes of drought, of wetting by salt spray, of the sun's fierce assault, are exceptional forms of adaptation and survival. The sands from which they grow shift and move with the motion of wind and sea, providing an open arena and a challenge to life of a special kind.

Every grain of sand on the beach has had a long history. Before it became sand it was rock, fractured by frost and by tree roots, ground by advancing glaciers and the waves, fractured again, and polished by the surf. Thus every beach is made up of those minerals that are naturally accessible, either blown from inland rocks or carried there by water. In Newfoundland some beaches are the dark gray of the local slate. In Nova Scotia, red beaches take their color from the sandstone of which they are largely composed. The "sandy beach" at Acadia National Park in Maine is about sixty per cent quartz; the remaining forty per cent is largely shell fragments, which give it an odd texture, granular but at the same time a little reminiscent of sawdust.

Along most of the North Atlantic, though, sandy beaches are made up principally of light-colored quartz grains, plus an assortment of other minerals that usually amount to no more than a tenth of the total mass of sand grains at the beach. Quartz is the most abundant mineral in the rocks of the northern part of the continent, as well as the toughest—the most likely to survive grinding and buffeting and to endure on the beach in the form of transparent grains, hard enough to scratch glass with. Other minerals in the rocks do not survive to such an extent. In fact, it is their disintegration by weathering that has freed the quartz grains in the first place, allowing them to be swept away by streams and rivers and ultimately to reach the shore.

Feldspar is also light in color (usually tan or gray), but it is easily told from quartz by its lack of glassy luster. Running a magnet through the sands will collect dark grains of two kinds, magnetite and ilmenite. Hornblende is also dark, usually deep green or, black, and may be found in long, thin fragments that resemble small petrified blades of grass. Certain dark particles in a handful of sand, examined under a low-powered microscope, will be seen to glisten like gems of deep purplish red. These are garnets, whose larger fragments can be used for jewelry. That the smaller fragments are used in making sandpaper is a testimony to the abrasive quality of wind-blown sand. Much rarer minerals are occasionally encountered among the sand grains, such as purple amethyst, rose quartz, tourmaline, topaz, and even sapphire.

Each of the different kinds of minerals usually occurs with other grains of the same kind, because of a selective sorting by the wind—which explains why a beach may be streaked with black or green, pink or white. Winds may be powerful enough to blow the quartz grains higher up on the beach, but not to sweep away those of heavier minerals, and so they are left as separate, distinctly colored patches. Relative wind velocities do their own sorting, giving a subtlety to the coloring of a beach made up of apparently uniform sand grains. Nor are these sand grains uniform in shape or size. Their variety tells their history. Grains that have been tossed about by the winds over sand dunes are usually frosted from the sandblasting they receive. Waterborne grains are usually more rounded, and often smaller, than the grains found on the upper beach.

**Sea Rocket**

A sand grain is relatively irreducible, having reached about the smallest size it can attain in the process of erosion, although under certain conditions it may be reduced to particles of silt or mud. It is protected against being ground down any further by the film of water which surrounds it, acting as a sort of protective cushion. Ranging from coarse to fine in texture, sand grains are smaller than eight-hundredths of an inch but larger than two-thousandths of an inch in size. No individual grains remain in the same place for very long, and, of course, the smaller they are the more easily they can be moved about. The heavier grains are likely to be found on the upper part of a beach and the finer sands in the lower parts, or in areas that are relatively sheltered from the waves. The same effect may be seen on many boulder beaches, where the heavier material may be found at the top and the smaller stones below. A beach like this, often forming a narrow but massive ridge, is continually being reshaped by the waves, the stones rolled down and displaced but then pushed back up again; and where the waves hit the beach at an angle they form pockets in the bank, which are in general the equivalent of longer curves and pockets along a sandy beach. The analogy, though valid, is limited because of the greater freedom of the sand with respect to wave motion. Each wave, depending on whether it is low or high, on its periodic relation to the waves that follow it, on its energy and the angle at which it approaches the shore, has its own characteristic effect on the beach.

In the local process of erosion, the sea carries and knocks boulders together day after day, hour after hour, taking fragments from them, reducing and rounding them. It grinds smaller stones together in massive quantities. Rock above the surf can be eroded by sand grains themselves that have been carried a few feet above the ground by strong wind. Waves also erode rocky cliffs by forcing water between cracks and trapping air inside them. As a result of compression, the air may have enough power to push fragments and sections of rock out into the sea.

On glaciated gravel or sandstone shores, made of looser material, storm waves may undermine the cliffs so that the stones,
gravel, and clay are displaced to become part of the beach or to be
transported by offshore currents. Where sand is abundant, its
particles are in motion in a perpetual exchange on and offshore.
The berm, that main part of the beach which is above water and
holds the bodies and the umbrellas, trades its sands, transported
by waves, with underwater bars that may be revealed only at low

Seabeach Sandwort or Sea Purslane

tide. In some instances the shifting of bars and the berm is a very elaborate and complex process, from season to season and from storm to storm, ranging in steepness and volume of sand from one area to another. Between spring and fall the beach builds up, or rather the part of it that is called the berm becomes wide, and more extensive, inclining gradually toward the water. Severe autumn and winter storms may cut into this fairly even volume of sand, narrowing the upper beach until it becomes little more than a high ledge in some places, with a steep slope below it. The relatively gentle waves of summer have only a minimal effect, but the storm waves that begin with the season of hurricanes do huge violence to the malleable sands. The effect of waves on any one kind of beach shifts with its nature and with the seasons, and the pattern of a flat and wide berm for summer and a steep and narrow one for winter may not always apply. Storm waves can level a beach in whole or part, as well as cave it away.

The more exposed sandy beaches, like Cape Cod's Outer Beach, are nearly barren. No less than the cobblestone beaches on stormy North Atlantic shores, they are rough and turbulent places—even more so, in fact, since they are almost in constant motion, with every lick and slap of a wave, every change in the tide. Stinging wastes of sand often blow down the surface of the beach, each grain, brown, black or crystal, shining and flying on its own. Little white beachfleas or sandhoppers find shelter here, as well as a few other crustaceans. The beachfleas, found on both exposed and sheltered shores, are interesting transitional animals. Like the rough periwinkles which have nearly crossed the boundary between sea and land on the rocky shore, these active little creatures of the sandy shore have already severed most of their ties to the water; their descendants appear destined for life on dry land. Thus far in their evolution they have crossed the high-tide mark, becoming one of the comparatively few crustaceans to live out of the sea, though they are still bound to it in certain respects.

The beachflea is abroad principally at night, and only with a falling tide. It leaves its burrow in the dry sands out of reach of the highest tides and makes its way to the tidal zone to feed on the jetsam left by the ebbing waters—bits of crab shells, dead fish, pieces of seaweed, remains of both plants and animals. It forms part of a community of scavengers at the high-tide line that also includes beetles, flesh flies, and worms.

The beachflea's other common name, sandhopper, is an apt one. If it must move to a new feeding ground, or if it senses danger, with a snap it suddenly straightens its body, which is normally bent, thus propelling itself several feet into the air. Before the full light of dawn, or before the tide rises again, all the beachfleas on the shore retreat to the area above high tide. There each digs its own burrow, a new one every day, and seals it shut with a sand door. Burrows with beachfleas still inside them are hard to find, except at the rare times when they are seen digging during daylight hours. Small holes often seen during the day on the upper beach are usually from the previous day, and no longer occupied.

On the exposed beaches, sea water held around the sand grains allows a certain number of minute animals such as worm larvae, nematode worms, rotifers, and copepods to exist. Driftwood provides at least temporary shelter for some animals, but even seaweed is relatively scarce, since what drifts in is later washed away by storm waves. A great deal of the life on an exposed beach is nonresident, coming from the land or arriving there briefly from less turbulent areas offshore. Many marine invertebrates whose empty shells may be found there are residents of the ocean bottom at depths of forty feet or more.

In the winter when the wind blows hardest, sea waters green and cold end as long lines of plumed waves falling, retreating, and conflicting on the beach. The sand under wind, and with the sea motion heavy alongside, seems to seethe, and run expansively on its own. Snow buntings land in white flocks on cliffsides and in the beach grass on top. An occasional snowy owl waits in the grass for mice, flying off when disturbed, long white wings beating surely and steadily, flicking slightly upward at the tips, into distant lighted waters and high clouds.

A beach that is not narrowly confined to the space between the bottom of a cliff and the sea, or completely exposed to the Atlantic, will naturally be a host to more varied and numerous kinds of life. Even the most sheltered shores can be severely altered by storm waves and winds, but their beaches are more often stable, remaining much the same from day to day despite the constant shifting and sorting of the sand grains of which they are composed; for each grain dislodged, another arrives to take its place. Protection by bays, within the irregular contours of the coastline, allows the growth of onshore grasses and weeds. There is no abrupt transition to the churning offshore depths. The shallower and warmer waters off such beaches give access to more kinds of marine life. But even protected beaches have the character of fringe environments, exposed to the extremes of both land and sea. Sand and its masses belong to the workings of the wind, and above all to surf and tide, storm waves, gentle liftings by the summer swells, and to currents, and ebb and flow of daylight, of seasons, of innumerable lives. The sandy beach, though a mere lip of the land, and not a major feature of the coast, becomes that part of the coast most allied to fluidity.

The blowing and sorting of sand grains by the wind may also build up dunes, although they are rare along the northeast coast where few beaches contain the huge volume of sand a dune requires. On Cape Cod there are dunes of considerable extent, and there is another well-known dune area at Castle Neck, inland from Crane's Beach, at Ipswich. Dunes are in essence the extension of a beach, rising above it on the inland side, with marshes behind, and they are usually located on former sand spits. Their birth came

BEACH
GRASS

BEACH
PEA

DUSTY
MILLER

**Dune Plants**

after long eras of sand accumulation. When the body of sand they came from reached sufficient dimensions so that its upper levels were dried out for most of the year, the sand grains began to be blown inland, and any projection—a piece of driftwood or a clump of beach grass—caused the wind to slow down and deposit them. In this way a small pile was formed whose dimension was gradually added to by winds carrying sands over the surface of the ground. After a while a considerable mound developed, with the characteristic shape of a foredune, a gentle slope facing the prevailing wind, a crest and steep slope at its back; in short, a wave sculptured in sand.

If, under such conditions, the winds are constant and there are no high obstacles such as cliffs or trees to break up their flow, the dune may now begin to migrate inland. Dunes on the march, like those on the tip of Cape Cod near Provincetown, may advance at a rate of ten to fifteen feet a year. Sand streams up the longer slope from the direction of the wind, is carried over the crest and falls down out of the wind to gather on the downwind face. When this slope becomes too steep to hold, the sand corrects its equilibrium by breaking off and falling down to the bottom of the dune; then the sand accumulates again to steepen the slope, and there is a constant transfer from one side of the dune to the other, with the result that it keeps on rolling forward.

The migration of the dunes of Provincetown and elsewhere is the product of an uneasy balance among the dunes themselves, the plants that anchor them, and the destructive power of the wind—plus man's mistreatment of the land. When European settlers first saw Cape Cod, most of the larger dunes were stabilized by pine, by shrubs, and by beach grass. But the settlers cut down the scanty woods and thickets for fuel and for building, and they turned their livestock loose to pasture on the dunes, trampling and devouring the plants. The destruction of a single plant can open a chink in the protective armor of vegetation that caps the dune, and soon there is enough loose sand so that it begins to blow. It piles over the plants on neighboring dunes, eventually destroying this anchoring vegetation, too, thus allowing the sand to blow. Moving sand has also buried forests of pitch pines, whose contorted tops can still be seen no more than a yard or two above the surface, like a dwarf forest. If these pines do manage to increase the height of their crowns faster than the dunes can grow, the chances are good that they will survive burial to continue living after the dunes that buried them have passed once more.

By the early decades of the last century, tree cutting and pasturing on the Cape Cod dunes had been forbidden by law; but it was too late to save the Provincetown dunes. Much of Cape Cod's tip had now been converted into nearly eight square miles of billowing sand: houses were buried by it, and it swept through the streets to such an extent that no one could walk through the town without feeling its bite, or tracking it home with him. "Nevertheless," wrote Henry David Thoreau in 1849, "natives of Provincetown assured me that they could walk in the middle of the road without trouble even in slippers, for they had learned how to put their feet down and lift them up without taking in any sand." This was the town, so he said, where in some pictures the persons of the inhabitants are not drawn below the ankles, so much being supposed to be buried in the sand. Much of the damage has now been mended by the construction of a long dike to protect the harbor from being filled in by sand, and by plantings, particularly of beach grass, on the dunes.

Beach grass and poverty grass are usually the first plants to take hold on a dune without vegetation, but, unless there is a replenishment of new sand, after a few years they will exhaust the nutrients in the soil and die. However, it is usual for the winds to keep piling new grains on top of old; and as the level of the dune rises, these grasses grow new rootstocks that enable them to keep their leaves above the sand. Year after year the growth and death of leaves and stems, the far-reaching roots that bind sand grains together, combine to make humus, which hastens the process of converting the inert mineral particles into true soil, capable of nurturing larger plants and of retaining water for a longer period of time.

A dune where a steady accretion of sand allows beach grass to take hold and other vegetation to follow will soon be covered with bayberries, beach plums, *rugosa* roses, and black cherries. The stage is now set for the invasion of pitch pine seedlings blown in from nearby woodlands. The humus created by the dune plants retains moisture, and the shrubs and flowering plants shelter the pine seedlings. The pitch pines soon put on height, and in the light reaching the dune between their outspread branches, other plants take hold, such as huckleberries, woodbine, poison ivy, and hazelnut. The dune will probably never progress beyond this point, but if it survives being smothered by sand, and if its pines are not toppled by storms, the pines will yield to oaks in a century or two. The dune will then be a rooted hill in its own right, assaulted by winds and salt spray, but no longer on the march.

The unstabilized, flowing dune country, like the regions of the beach, has its particular demands and conditions in which life can exist, even though its sheer slopes and surfaces are glaring and inhospitable. The sands are usually dry on the surface and sometimes rub together, making an eerie singing sound in the wind. When the wind blows harder, a thick mist of sand grains travels a few feet above the dune, polishing the knotted trunks of pine and pitting the leaves of dune plants. The surface is baked by the sun, and moisture may be six inches or more below it. All the same, sand is not necessarily unfriendly to life, as can be seen on the upper levels of a beach. Sand grains there are held together by what moisture they receive, particularly from the dew, so that they do not often blow at night. Seepage takes place, so that water does not run off, and there is thus little erosion. So unless they are being assaulted and moved forward by fall and winter winds, the dunes are stable for the time being. Trees and thickets grow on their periphery, from which animals such as skunks and foxes make marauding visits, hunting grubs and mice, and the bottoms of hollows between them may be close enough to the water table to provide moisture for wild cranberries and bog-loving plants, areas which can nurture a meadow mouse. Toads are occasionally found in the dunes or wandering to the far edge of the beach. Marsh hawks live there on white-footed mice, deer mice, jumping mice, shrews, and cottontails that frequent pockets of low-growing trees and shrubs. The tracks of mice show on the dunes, along with circles inscribed by beach grass and the designs left by dead sticks or beach-grass roots tumbling down a slope before the wind. Pencil-sized holes reveal the nesting places of wolf spiders, which carry their young on their backs while hunting. These wolf spiders are pale in color, blending with the sand and not easily noticed where they wait for a stray insect to pass near their burrows. The dune grasshopper is camouflaged in a similar way.

In a particular area, one dune may have become relatively stabilized by natural processes; another may be held down or slowed in its course by beach-grass plantings while an adjoining dune is slowly moving downwind, menacing trees and plants along its way. A coastal dune is not uniform, but has its pockets of life, some more hospitable than others. Life clusters in protected hollows, near damp places, and on the decaying tissues of buried pines, or of beach plums, cherries, and quaking aspen. Sometimes toadstools of unlikely kinds can be found growing in the dunes. Mushrooms and toadstools usually require an abundance of moisture and would not be expected in dry sand, but several kinds do grow there, given enough decayed material for their nourishment. The most easily recognized of the mushrooms is one called the earth star, which has a top like a puffball; its enveloping outer layer is divided into pointed segments which during wet weather unfold like petals, but in dry spells curl up to protect the center.

Just as there is an aspect of suspended flow about the sand dunes, a migration in slow time, so they and other sandy seashore regions are in their way a reminder of periods in the distant past when major earth and coastal changes took place. The glaciers are less hard to visualize once we have become accustomed to looking for their evidence. The results, in scratched rock, sloping plains, rounded knolls, and piles of miscellaneous material, are all around us. On a glaciated shore with gravelly banks and beaches, with ice cakes moving between fingers of water and empty sand in the wintertime, it is possible to imagine an era when the glacier was retreating. The landscape was large and barren, strewn with glacial rubble, great ridges of debris, with cold air still standing in from ice to the north, mists floating like smoke after a major devastation, and the winds whipping bare sand and piling it up into barrows and dunes, while the sea ebbed and flowed through an expanse of spits and shoals and islands. In some parts of the coast there are wind-carved stones called ventifacts, whose sheer faces are the result of lying exposed to those cold, sand-driving winds for thousands of years. Pick one up and you touch a prolongation of time. Just as beach grass reaches far and deep for moisture and thus holds the sand in place, so other plants take their opportunity when it comes. Vegetation returned after the glaciers, and trees rerooted, when the climate was propitious; for whenever an environment changes so that it is favorable to the growth of a plant, the plant moves in with alacrity. Travel of seeds by wind and water, and in the alimentary tracts of birds, is fast in any event, but whatever the method and rate of travel, all plants carry in them the potential of migration to a new but appropriate environment. Plants profit by change when the change suits them; they grow and compete, fighting hard for existence until such time as the environment changes again and is hostile to them.

Snowy Owl

To see a familiar plant in a different location—the crowberry, for example, growing with the low tundralike vegetation of Newfoundland, after you have seen it in the Jersey pine barrens, or on Cape Cod sands—is not only to begin to understand the ranges of geologic time, but also to get an inkling of the worldwide lodgings of plants and animals. This is no man's home plant, to be tended, captured, or claimed. It is the earth's, and its growth and migration are both behind and ahead of us. The northeast coast is in it, with an ageless swing and momentum, and its countless lives seizing their outward chances.

# TIDAL GROUNDS

**6**

THE FLATS BEYOND a sandy beach at low tide are probably one of the most inscribed areas on the face of the earth. Aside from ripples on the sand, and rill marks—fine-veined drainage channels made by retreating tides along the beach or by springs of water issuing from the land—pools and runnels stretch off to the horizon between the brown-ribbed sands, whisked or whipped by the wind, reflecting the moon and the sun in all their passages. There is silver in the springtime and at dawn, copper at sundown, and fiery orange, white, and purple in the wintertime colors.

During the winter, ripple marks not covered by blocks of pack ice or ridges of snowy ice pushed in by the tide are likely to be semi-frozen into heavy, chainlike patterns. Signs of life are infrequent except for the footprints of gulls. At other seasons the sand is marked universally with some evidence of habitation or passing things. Aside from marks made by waves, and the water birds of different seasons, the signs at the lower beach are mostly of life in hiding. Instead of thick glistening mats of seaweed, holding in their fronds numerous animals attached to the rocks or to the weeds themselves, instead of tidepools and crevices and sea caves, the sandy shore revealed at low tide appears barren. Life on and within the sand grains is not only different from life on the rocks, it is also more limited in the number of individuals and species of plants and animals; and it also requires a different set of adaptations. The sandy beach offers no solid support for the attachment of holdfasts or for sessile organisms such as barnacles, mussels, and sponges. The multitudes of crabs and starfishes that can find refuge from sun and wind in rocky crevices when the tide is out are relatively absent on sandy shores, though it may be added that protected shores of the kind where tidal flats occur are seldom without their share of rocks and stones.

Despite their seeming hardships, the sands do offer hospitable conditions for certain kinds of plants and animals. Since it lacks the sharp irregularities of the rocky shore, a beach affords largely uniform conditions all along it with respect to drying out, wave action, or length of exposure between the tides. Sand is also a barrier to sharp changes in temperature and salinity; moisture can always be found merely by burrowing a few inches beneath the surface. Very few organisms can be found on top of the sands except when the tide is in, and so the life of the sands is the life *within* them. Burrowing is the key to survival, enabling an animal to get away from extreme changes in salinity or temperature and to escape wave action, predators, or drying out between the tides.

Where there is a muddy substratum or beds of peat, some seaweed may be able to take hold, such as the bladder wrack; and the beach will have a litter of Irish moss, kelp, and rockweed from farther waters. The flats may have an intermittent growth of eelgrass or "sea grass," which has the rare distinction of being both a marine plant and a flowering one. Its ribbonlike leaves extend to a length of eight feet, and the tresses grow in dense masses that give excellent shelter to all kinds of marine life—young fish, snails, clams, brittle stars, sea anemones, stalked jellyfish, and pipefish, jungles for whole communities of the preying and the preyed upon. But the eelgrass grows in nothing like the quantity it once did. It was apparently attacked by a parasite—though weather cycles have also been blamed—and after 1931 great beds of it disappeared along the Atlantic coast; in fact, it was almost destroyed on both sides of the Atlantic, although it survived along Mediterranean and Pacific shores, and it is only now returning in a number of areas along the northeast coast.

Eelgrass flourished in sheltered waters, where it was rooted in muddy sand, and it was especially thick at the mouths of tidal creeks and estuaries. In fact, some fishermen used to call it the "tiresome weed," since it entangled their oars and slowed the movement of their boats. Still, its disappearance—and for once man may congratulate himself on not being to blame—was disastrous not only for many species of marine life such as scallops, clams, and shrimps, but also for the flocks of brant that fed upon it. Within only a few years the brants fell to a fraction of their former numbers, but they began to readjust to a diet of sea lettuce and other algae and made a substantial comeback. The decline of the eelgrass beds produced a marked slump in scallop fisheries along the coast, and the scallops have been slow to return. In addition, its leaves sheltered crustaceans, fishes, and many species of invertebrate life that deposited their eggs there, all of which suffered drastic declines in number. When the eelgrass went, its long ramifying roots lost their hold on the bottom of coves and

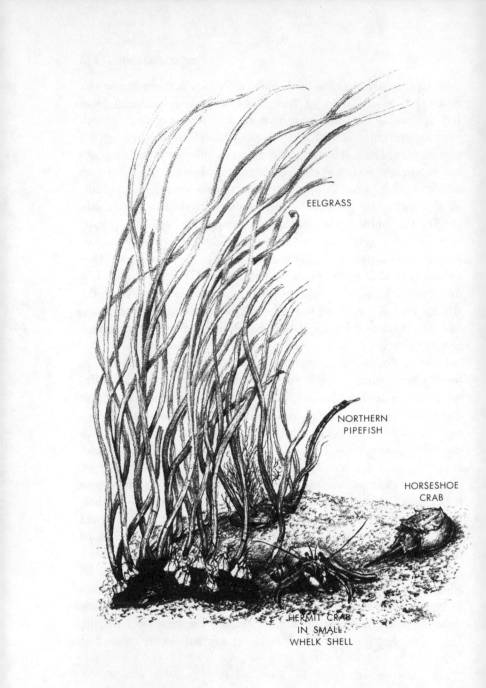

EELGRASS

NORTHERN
PIPEFISH

HORSESHOE
CRAB

HERMIT CRAB
IN SMALL
WHELK SHELL

bays, with the result that well-rooted plants were swept away and replaced by shifting sands, and in the process a great many clam and oyster beds were smothered.

It is interesting to note that the loss of the eelgrass had some minor effect on human economy. Massive amounts of it were piled up on many beaches after autumn and winter storms. Of these masses, tons were rolled in tough, tangled windrows which caught and held drifting sand, adding to the substance of the beach, absorbing the shock of the surf, and helping to check erosion along the shoreline. Cape Codders called it "seaweed" as opposed to kelp and what they called "quill stuff"—other forms of algae such as are usually lumped under the heading of seaweed. They transported it in oxcarts and farm wagons to pack as insulation around the foundations of their houses, and they stuffed it between the eighteen-inch insulating space that separated the inner and outer walls of an ice house. (These ice houses in a non-electric age were extremely important in preserving salable fish caught in offshore weirs.) Eelgrass was also processed commercially for house insulation, soundproofing, and mattresses. Stacks of it stood in every barnyard for use in bedding down the livestock, and it was mixed with manure and spread on meadows.

All along the crescent of tidal flats on Cape Cod Bay, for example, beginning at least a mile out, there was an increasingly compact plateau of eelgrass sod as a walker approached the shore, sinking ankle-deep into the slender, slippery, dark-green ribbons each lying as the ebb tide had left it, pointing toward the nearest little meandering channel. The dense submarine meadow reached inshore almost to the foot of the beaches, remaining under water at even the lowest low tides, and rippling in the sunlit currents with a dancelike motion. The effect of the plateau of rooted eelgrass was to give stability to the tidal flats and protection to the shellfish that wintered there, since winter icepacks slid over its surface instead of plowing it up.

These eelgrass surfaces were characterized by what the local inhabitants called "salt holes," ranging from shallow pockmarks to irregular pools a foot or two in depth, always full of clear salt water even when the tide was lowest. Thus the eelgrass meadow had its own natural aquariums, its own tidepools, as full of marine animals as those on rocky shores. Lobsters used salt holes to burrow under the overhanging banks, with exits a yard or so to the rear. They would leave telltale heaps of sand on the bottom, and the way to catch one was to poke into the entrance of its sand burrow and watch carefully for the stir it made as it backed out the exit under the deep tangle of covering eelgrass.

In addition to flounder, scallops, eels, mussels, crabs, shrimp, hermit crabs, and many other species for which eelgrass meant pasturage and protection, it also sheltered large numbers of soft-shell clams. Natives are inclined to blame the disappearance of the soft-shells, also called steamers and long-necks, on the loss of the eelgrass. There is nothing to prove that it was indispensable for their production, however. The decline of the soft-shell began some time before the eelgrass went. Rather, the decline seems to be correlated with reckless harvesting, though in recent years pollution may have also contributed. In Maine, where soft-shells have always been more abundant than in Massachusetts, there has also been a serious decline. The causes include bad digging practices—such as crushing and burying young clams with rakes—pollution of intertidal water, an increase in northern waters of the predatory green crab, and excessive exploitation. The decline of the eelgrass does not seem to have been critical, since the soft-shell can use many different kinds of areas—mud, sand, gravel, bars at the mouths of creeks—in which to "set."

All the same, it is true that the eelgrass provided concealment and good ground to grow in for the adult clams of this species and that they grew to considerable size where they were embedded, a foot or so down, siphoning in water and food with long "necks" stretching above the surface. These siphons enable the soft-shell clam to stay beneath the surface and to become more deeply embedded as they grow in length. A large adult might be six inches long and three inches wide, making it the staple "chowder clam." When the tide ebbed, a digger for soft-shell clams dyked off an area of a few square feet with eelgrass sod to prevent the water from draining in, and he might dig "a barrel to a tide." The spawn of the soft-shell were pushed inshore by the tides and lodged among the roots of the saltwater grass, called "sage grass" in parts of New England, apparently a pronunciation of "sedge." There the young began to grow, being at the surface to begin with, holding on with byssus threads, replenishing what used to be thought of as an inexhaustible supply.

The bivalve mollusks, such as the soft-shell and other clams, are among the animals best adapted for life in the sands. Their flattened shells enable them to cut through the sands as easily as with a knife; equipped with long siphons or "necks" they can stay hidden while drawing food from the surface; and the large gill chamber located within the space of the two shells permits a high rate of respiration in the clogged environment of sand and mud.

The most specialized of the bivalves is the razor-shell clam, found from Labrador southward. Its narrow shell grows to a length of about seven inches and resembles the handle of a barber's razor. It can often be found standing upright in the sand near the low-water mark; but to sight a razor-shell is not the same as to catch it. If disturbed, even by vibrations, the animal disappears with amazing rapidity into the sands, pulled downward by its enormous foot, which when retracted may occupy half the interior of the shell. Some people try to outdig a razor-shell, but a much less tiring way is to drop a handful of salt over the depression at the top of its burrow; the increased salinity will irritate the clam sufficiently to make it come to the surface. Even if one manages, by slicing through the sand, to dig out a razor-shell faster than it is able to get away, it is still likely to escape the hand that grasps it by using the power of its muscular foot like a steel spring.

Immense refuse mounds or kitchen middens left by the Indians could once be found all along the northeastern shore, before a growing population overwhelmed the region with housing and asphalt pavement. The largest of these middens, at Damariscotta, Maine, contained some seven million bushels of shells. Most of these came from a bivalve known in its smaller stages as the cherrystone clam, then as the littleneck, and finally, when grown to full size, as the quahog or hard-shell clam. Pick up one of the shells of this common species and you will usually find that the inside has a purple or dark blue border. It was from this part of the quahog's shell that the Indians fashioned beads of the valuable purple wampum. White beads were fashioned also from a variety of shells, including periwinkles and whelks, but they were much less valuable than the purple ones. The Europeans loosely used the word wampum to mean any kind of shell money, but for the Algonkian tribes the original meaning was of sacred significance. It was only after the arrival of the settlers that the wampum necklaces, belts, and decorative rows on clothing came to be used for tribute, for ransoming captives, and in written records (such as the wampum treaty belt, symbolizing the agreement between the Penn family and the Indians of Pennsylvania). In the early years of European settlement, shell beads were accepted as a standard of value; their use spread from the Algonkians to the Iroquois of the interior, and eventually almost to the Rocky Mountains. Their manufacture, however, was greatly facilitated by the use of the white man's metal tools, which led to an oversupply and devaluation, so that shell currency was soon replaced by metal coins.

Wherever there are clam beds, it is possible to see a hill of sand moving just under the surface. Scoop it up and you will find the shell of a moon snail, plowing a path with its enormous muscular foot. The speed of this snail is not very great, but its movements are persistent, and sooner or later it will cross the path of a clam. The moon snails usually seen on tidal flats are a smaller species, whose chief prey is the soft-shell clam, though it will also attack its own kind; but between the low-tide line and deep water lives a species with a shell as large as a man's fist and a foot which may be ten inches long, a giant that feeds primarily on quahogs and surf clams. The moon snail's method of feeding is to enfold the shell of its victim with its foot, and then to drill a neat hole with its radula, a rasplike ribbon of closely-set teeth, aided by a glandular secretion of sulphuric acid that eats away the hard parts of the shell. Then the moon snail uses the radula to scrape out the inner tissues of its victim, passing them back into its gizzard.

In those seasons when the inhabitants of tidal flats are not hidden deep to escape ice and cold, the surface reveals their signs everywhere, often for miles along sheltered shores. There are innumerable holes, as well as small mounds, coiled castings of sand, meandering burrows, paths lightly inscribed by passing snails, tracks wandering over ridges and down the troughs of sand, and even occasional tracks made by stones buoyed up by seaweed. The sand itself when closely inspected may prove not only to be sand-colored, but to be covered, and even impregnated several inches deep, with tiny bits of green algae. All these surface signs are a part of a tidal expansion and contraction, an erasing and re-inscribing, a coming in and going out.

The common periwinkle is one of the relatively few animals to be seen out in the open. It was originally confined to Europe, but was probably introduced to North America by man, possibly the Norse settlers who brought it over in their boats. Whether they did or not, the periwinkle is a vegetarian of many environments, hiding in wet rockweed on rocky shores, moving over tidal sands to feed on algae. Common periwinkles do not cling like barnacles and limpets, but are relatively loose and easily dislodged. They go with a current and not against it, surviving storms, as it were, by rolling with the punches. On tidal flats the smaller periwinkles are swept away by light currents that tumble them over and over. Others travel down the middle of ripple troughs, sometimes in single file when the sands are damp and not covered by water, their shells rolling from side to side.

So, in their wanderings, moving very slowly, antennae extended, they are dispersed along the shore, but they usually return more or less to where they started from. They are equipped with no particular skill in finding their way back, nor do they have an unusual memory; it is, rather, a compromise between several behavioral pulls and tugs that draws them back to their accustomed places. The common periwinkle is born with a tendency to move upward on the beach against the force of gravity, and it also displays a predilection for warmth. The effect of these two drives is to send a periwinkle gliding away from the sea to less chilly and higher ground. The upward movement is counteracted, however, by an aversion to drying out, which at a certain degree conquers the negative response to gravity. As a result the periwinkle stops, and by then it is usually in its accustomed zone. When a periwinkle is swept toward the low-tide line, the wetting triggers the negative response to gravity and sends it climbing up the shore until it becomes sufficiently dried out to respond positively to gravity. The combined result of gravity, temperature, and wetting or drying is to bring the periwinkle back to the beach zone characteristic of its species, the zone from which it started before being dislodged by the waves.

A stone that has been buoyed by seaweed fronds enough to be lifted and bumped along by tidal waters may carry along with it a few barnacles—helpless in their tenacity—and a few amphipods that skip sideways or swim off when disturbed. The color of amphipods may be olive-green like seaweed, yellow-green, dark brown, reddish-brown, or even transparent. They have bodies that are flattened from side to side—rather than from top to bottom like the isopods, crustaceans similar to the common pillbugs or sowbugs on land—and they swim, flit, jump, and wiggle on wet weeds, with a nervous agitation typical of their kind. Sand shrimps, the kind that flick over your bare feet, are so adapted to the sand that they seem almost to swim in it. Speckled and semi-transparent, they are able to burrow in the sand very rapidly by means of their legs and swimming appendages, beating away the sand and settling down into it.

Another sand traveler is a small animal known as *Chirodotea caeca*, whose burrows, just under the surface, make meandering ridges over the flats, gentle raised trails. The careful watcher may see one of these burrows being constructed, and pick out the animal as it moves. This is an isopod, with a gray, segmented or plated body, flat and domed on its upper side, with a round, blunt prow and pointed rear. Thanks to its sixteen constantly wiggling legs, it is equipped to move through the surface sands at a fair rate of speed.

The two terrains of sand and mud are not easily separated. On any stretch of shore, the animals that are adapted to one or another or a mixture of both will vary greatly in number and kind, and any such environment may go through extensive changes from season to season or even from day to day. Storms may carry away great volumes of surface sand, leaving muddy flats; or waves and currents may do just the opposite, sweeping sands over peat beds, silt, or mud. Bivalves such as quahogs, soft-shells, and scallops may dwindle in abundance not only because of exploitation but also because of changes in the tidal ground. Each long shore, each small crescent bay, has its own conditions for a whelk, a slipper shell, or a worm.

Mud is usually deposited only where there is little wave action or other movement of water—except in an estuary, where a heavy supply of silt is brought down to the shore by the movement of a river. Even in an estuary, though, the muddier areas will be the sheltered ones. The life of the mudflat is quite different from that in any other shore habitat. The substratum, made up of fine particles smaller than the smallest sand grains, is extremely yielding; unless shells or stones are mixed with it, there is no support for seaweed holdfasts or the sessile shells of barnacles, mussels, and limpets. On the other hand, burrowing is easy in the soft texture of mud, and there are many specialized burrowing forms that can live in this clogging environment. There is no sharp dividing line between the animals of sand and mud, but rather a graduated series of differences. In examining the bivalves of the northeastern coast, it is possible to distinguish species that inhabit sand, sandy mud, pure mud, and many gradations in between. In areas of nearly pure sand, large cockle or heart shells abound. As the sand be-

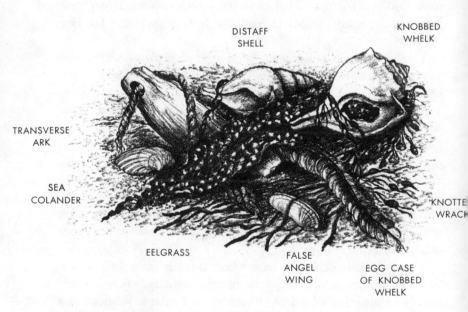

DISTAFF SHELL

KNOBBED WHELK

TRANSVERSE ARK

SEA COLANDER

KNOTTE WRACK

EELGRASS

FALSE ANGEL WING

EGG CASE OF KNOBBED WHELK

**Tide Line**

comes mixed with a little more mud, small wedge shells appear, to such an extent that enough of the clams that inhabit them can be dug to make chowder, in spite of their small size. When the substratum is about half sand and half mud, quahogs or littlenecks will be found, and when it is almost completely mud the most common bivalve is apt to be the stubby razor-clam.

Burrowing enables an animal to survive the mud, but it poses problems for survival also. An animal several inches or a foot below the surface must develop a way to feed without losing the benefit of being sheltered. Four primary methods which have been developed by animals of the sand and mud habitat may be seen in the worms that spend most of their lives under the surface. One method is that of the suspension feeders. When the tide is high,

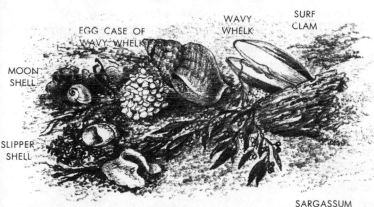

**After Storm**

these worms draw in water from the surface and feed on its tiny floating plants and animals. Such a feeder is the ornate tubeworm, which builds fairly thick tubes of sand grains and mud, from which its feeding tentacles extend to beat in the microscopic organisms of sea water. Its body is a glowing persimmon red or pinkish orange. Along the many waving, flesh-colored tentacles are three pairs of shorter, blood-red gills; the sight of all these suddenly spread out, after you have dislodged a worm from its tube, can be disconcerting, as if a flower had suddenly been torn loose.

A second method, known as deposit feeding, also works only when the tide is in. The worm extrudes the feeding end of its body from its burrow, collecting detritus and microscopic plants and animals from the surface. A trumpet worm, *Pectanaria gouldii*—it has no common name—builds shining cone-shaped tubes cemented together out of sand grains, selected and fitted with the utmost care, the large grains at the large end and the smaller ones at the other. As the short body of the worm carries its gracefully tapered house along, head down, it makes a burrow or vertical shaft below the surface, with the small end of the tube projecting above it. It feeds, to one side of the shaft, by passing sand out of the narrow end of the tube, in such a way that new material keeps falling down with a fresh supply of food. The worm's body is flesh-colored with red gill-like plumes on either side of its head which is also equipped, surprisingly enough, with two sets of projecting combs, pure gold in color, which it uses to dig its burrows with.

There are few other worms that show such precision, such perfect care, and art in their lives. Still, there are others of equal color and interest, like the plumed worm, found from southern New England to South Carolina, a large iridescent animal with a series of bright red gills branching from its head, which is drawn back quickly into its tube when touched by a mere shadow. These tubes can be very long, three feet or more. They are constructed of a parchmentlike material, and where they project above the surface, their top few inches are camouflaged with bits of seaweed, sticks, and shells. There are also worms to be found under the rocks and stones; others live inside or on the surface of stones and of empty shells. Some worms build tubes; other worms may burrow, in either mud or sand, instead of building tubes. The tiny *Spirorbis* worm even has a white, flattened, and coiled shell, a living tube of its own, and hundreds of these can be found encrusted on stones or fronds of seaweed.

The worms of the third group have largely liberated themselves from the tides, since they can feed in moist sand. Like the earthworms on land, they swallow immense amounts of sand and mud, digesting whatever organic matter is mixed with them, and excreting the rest. The most common of these is the lugworm, which is about as thick and as long as a pencil and is most abundant in sandy mud rather than in clean sand or pure mud. It swallows great quantities of this element, extracting only the small proportion that is edible, and depositing the remainder as a pile of coiled castings on the surface. A look at these castings, conspicuous features of the beach, will disclose shallow depressions close to them which lead into the shafts of the lugworm's burrow. The burrow itself is in the shape of a U. Its walls are strengthened with mucus and etched with marks left by the hooked bristles with which the worm grips them when it is moving. The worm usually lies in the central horizontal part of this burrow, gorging itself on sand at the head end. The continual withdrawal of sand from this end is what causes the telltale depression in the surface above. The lugworm never runs out of a supply of sand, for each incoming tide fills the depression with more for it to engorge.

Finally, the fourth method of feeding is that of the predators which temporarily abandon their burrows and swim in search of food. The common clam worm is large, thick-bodied, and voracious, as anyone who has been nipped by one can readily attest. Free-swimming during night hours, moving sinuously after its prey, it is itself a prey of fish; by day it burrows in sand or mud. In color it is steel-blue or dull-green tinged with flesh-color or orange, and it has a shimmering iridescence in the sunlight.

Where rivers, brooks, and creeks meet the sea they form the special and distinctive environment of the estuary, a transition zone between waters fresh and salt. Technically, an estuary is a baylike passage or other body of water in which a stream mixes with sea water and dilutes it. It comes within the range of this chapter because it carries sand, mud, and silt particles seaward over tidal grounds. Estuarial regions as a rule lack clean, sandy beaches, since stones or sand tend to collect silt. Mud, of varying textures, is the common material. But as a place for life, the estuary lacks the stability of a sheltered sandy or muddy shore. It is an environment of constant change caused by the opposition of fresh water currents and the tides. Salinities increase and decrease as a result, temperatures are being altered all day long, and sediments are stirred up so that illumination also varies.

Several kinds of animals, such as *Nephthys* worms and the delicate little *Macoma* shell, found in estuaries are also common to other shore habitats; but there are a number of others that are rarely found outside of estuaries, including a spire shell, one of the clam worms, and several crustaceans. A majority of the estuarial fauna are burrowers, particularly those with a high tolerance for the clogging effects of mud, or those able to burrow deep for protection against sudden changes in salinity and temperature. There are also several kinds of animals that invade the estuary at low tide, and still others that do so at high tide. As the waters retreat, large numbers of wading birds, such as plovers and ducks, descend on the mudflats, probing and sifting for mollusks and worms; and the tracks of rats and raccoons may be seen before the first morning tide obliterates them. During high water these animals retreat, and as the sea spreads up the estuarial bay, it brings with it various fishes, crabs, and shrimps, all of which move regularly in and out of the estuary with the tides.

One of the common marks of an estuary is the oyster bed, an assemblage of countless numbers of shells usually found near its seaward end. The life cycle of the oyster has become adjusted to the special conditions of an estuary, with its variously saline waters. Adult oysters live where the water is brackish, but the fragile larvae released into the sea must have a way to reach these same areas. Oysters in their youthful stage, just after hatching, drift helplessly back and forth with the currents that sweep toward the shore and then move back out to sea. But the main tendency is seaward, with the flow of water from the river augmenting that of the ebb tide. The larvae that manage to survive to the age of about two weeks, and that remain in the estuary, undergo a marked change. They no longer drift aimlessly but drop to the bottom on the ebb tide, and so avoid being carried out to sea. With the return of the flood tide, they rise and are swept upstream, proceeding along the estuary by stages until they reach water of a suitable brackishness.

To all the fluctuating and hazardous conditions for life in an estuary, man has added a new one. Pollutants, the by-products of his tenure on the land, affect estuaries and their natural lives in a number of ways. The pollutants in themselves may be toxic, or they may alter the natural balance of the water's constituents by decreasing the oxygen content. Waste settling on the bottom may clog the gills of oysters and other animals. Even without being smothered, oysters suffer from pollution, since the presence of certain substances in the water causes their shells to remain closed, so that the oysters do not feed during the favorable part of the tidal cycle and either starve or are greatly weakened if they survive.

Each tidal environment has a set of different opportunities for life, depending on its relative exposure to storm waves, on average temperatures, salinities, and illumination, on the kind of mud or sand, on the quantity of rocks along the shore. Any species, animal or plant, has its own requirements and sensitivities, its chance to function in narrow confinements perhaps, but as part of the great natural rhythms. Single lives are seen in manifold dimensions. So, way out on an offshore bar, where clear, green sea water breaks white over sand, frequented by men that dig for it on extreme neap tides, is the surf clam, measuring half a foot or more in length, sending up siphons to employ the cold food of the sea. The surf clam inhabits a stout shell, of classic whiteness, whose concentric lines of growth have the grandeur of all slow accretions —of chalk cliffs, coral reefs, and canyon walls.

Farther inshore, a pearly gray moon snail flowing forward, a small green crab digging backward into the sand, shrimps twitching and sending up quick clouds of sand, crimson worms writhing under a stone, minnows darting in sunny shallows . . . these, too, are classic in their particularity, through the long rhythms of the shore.

Tidal movements give them their cue, their call to hide or emerge. Night and day, and the seasons, have their immediate effects. Between waves, the sanderlings hurry after tiny crustaceans in the sand. Mottled ruddy turnstones move over stones to find food beneath them; the slender yellowlegs stand in shallow water, and sharp-bodied terns dive for small fish in the surface waters, or lift up from sand flats in a white cloud of stir and motion, as they sound their harsh trills. Great black-backed and herring gulls stand on sandy or muddy perimeters as a tide starts to turn lightly, flicking against the outgoing waters of a tidal inlet or estuary, rippling and foaming around the stems of shore grasses. The waters deepen. The gulls fly off down the shore. Fish stir in the gathering pools, then school and spread out. Barnacles open their shells and start feeding, as do the clams and mussels in

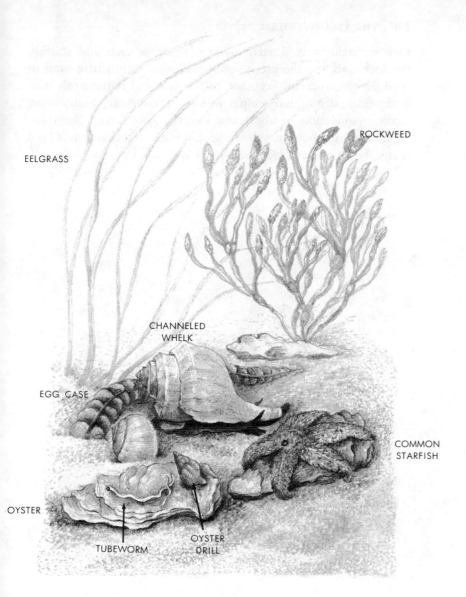

ROCKWEED

EELGRASS

CHANNELED
WHELK

EGG CASE

COMMON
STARFISH

OYSTER

TUBEWORM

OYSTER
DRILL

**Oysters with Predators**

their different ways. Predators—the horseshoe crab and starfish, the rock crab and the green crab—feed vigorously where sand or mud flats were recently exposed to the sun; and bottom fish such as flounder, skates, and sculpin move closer inshore. Many other feeding populations readjust and interchange between the tides. Countless impulses are at work, countless reactions, over and under the sandy or muddy margins of land and sea.

# THE SALT MARSH

**7**

SEACOAST MARSHES may have taken thousands of years to build, growing by slow progression during the post-glacial era when there was a gradual rising of the sea in relation to the land. What has been called the New England type of marsh occurs behind sandbars and barrier beaches, often in "drowned" areas formerly occupied by freshwater marshes and ponds. It can be differentiated from the other basic kind of marsh on the North Atlantic coast, such as that found at the Bay of Fundy, which consists primarily of silt or soft red mud with a great deal less vegetation.

A salt marsh begins its formation when the sea, by tidal action, deposits fine-grained sediment across bays and estuaries along the coast, fencing off shallow waters which fill in with silt. The resulting mudflats are then colonized by saltwater grasses. Different species of these grasses can tolerate various degrees of tidal submergence, beginning with saltwater cordgrass, which grows down from high-water level. Peat is built up by the successive, decaying

141

layers of its root masses and the accumulation of sediment, and as the sea level rises, the upper surface of the marsh rises with it. When the intertidal deposit of peat reaches high-water level, another kind of marsh vegetation succeeds the first, making new layers of peat on top of it. The resulting records of the different kinds of plant growth over the ages makes it possible to read the history of the land by sounding the marsh depths with rods and by collecting samples of peat from various levels.

Such a marsh is slow and measured in its growth. Starting with a few isolated pockets along an upland margin, it spreads and enlarges over thousands of years. What begins as a meandering channel system, a mere etching on tidal flats, sending out tongues and patches of moisture, begins to stabilize in a pattern of creeks and channels that are lengthened, defined, and deepened. A precise study of the Great Marsh at Barnstable, Massachusetts, has been made by Dr. Alfred C. Redfield of the Woods Hole Oceanographic Institution. He reconstructed its state at intervals as far back as 3,300 years ago showing that sea level was then about 18 feet lower than it is now.

Meandering channels may retain much the same form and position for centuries, although they do change their position slightly when sharp corners are rounded by fast currents, or they can be widened by "slumps" when peat breaks off their banks. A slump on one bank of a channel is usually balanced by an extension of grasses and sediment on the other, and in that way it is stabilized again, though its course may be shifted a few feet or yards in the process. A stream so shapes its channel that its water forces are distributed equally over all its parts, guaranteeing the least possible erosion and sustaining an equilibrium determined by the volume, depth, and velocity of the water it carries and by the rhythm of the tides.

Not all seaside marshes, of course, are strictly salt marshes. They may be dyked and banked and put beyond the reach of salt water. They may merge with brackish areas where the vegetation changes character, and extend even farther inland to freshwater marshes. Some marshes have been severed from the sea that brought them into being, and, fenced off by sandbars, have turned into freshwater swamps. They are found all along the coast in varying degrees of breadth and composition, stretching for many miles behind the protection of long sandspits or barrier beaches, or persisting as narrow fringes and small pockets here and there. Along some shorelines it is possible to see them in the process of building, the pioneering grasses standing out on tidal flats.

A salt marsh does not always need a thousand years to build. Given the right conditions, it may develop within a lifetime out of a sandflat or shallow bay, although it will lack the depth and stability of an older marsh. Patches of saltwater cordgrass may suddenly start growing, if there is an appropriate supply of sediment. First there is only sand; then a few dozen seedlings appear. The next year and the year following there will be more of these, growing somewhat higher. Then the grass will begin to collect between its stems the sand that washes in during the winter. During the summer the roots accumulate, and the new marsh area begins to build up, at a rate of about an inch a year. The process becomes much slower as the grasses grow thicker, making it harder for the washed-in sand to penetrate between them; and so the strata of accumulated sand will be thinner. This process continues until the surface of the marsh has risen to high-water level. In a matter of forty or fifty years you might see part of a sandflat turned into an island of salt marsh, or even a wide area growing productive crops of salt hay.

Despite the land developer's assurance, the possibility that new marshes may develop cannot, of course, be used as an excuse for the indiscriminate filling in of existing marshes, or of flats, coves, and bays. Just as eelgrass will not return along many shore bottoms changed or tampered with by cities, industry, and housing

CORDGRASS       MARSH HAWK

**A Salt Marsh**

developments, so marshes, too, need undisturbed areas in which to develop in their natural and time-honored way. Of the various kinds of coastal areas we now see, the salt marsh is probably most like what the original settlers found. It represents gradual and measured growth over the ages. It is unique and cannot be replaced, in the way that an inland area, completely denuded of its forests, can be replanted with trees. Salt marshes are unmatched assets, with strong ties to our own history, and a natural complexity and abundance which we have hardly started to measure. But the inroads made on them by "urban sprawl" have been very great. Thousands of acres have been erased by filling. Connecticut, for example, has already lost half of its useful tidal marshes, and in other states the measures taken to protect them have often been too little and too late, or they have been successfully by-passed and ignored.

Marshes have often been objected to because of their odor, but an ill-smelling marsh is likely to be either polluted or improperly drained. Nothing is better than the clean salt air blowing off undisturbed marshes. That their plant life has a high rate of decay and that they are continually washed by the tides guarantees the kind of decomposition and nutriment upon which the growth and the health of the community of life depend. Consider the lowly marsh snail, a little creature with a dark-brown shiny shell like a pellet rolled between your fingers. It is immediately dependent on organic decay for its life—and so, indirectly, is a great deal else, including ourselves.

The old culture of the coast, now being replaced except in parts of Canada, considered a marsh in terms of organic use. Farmers pastured cattle on it, and they used its grasses for salt hay, stacks of which were a common part of the coastal scene not so many years ago, and are still to be found in a few areas. Marsh-grown rushes were once woven into chairs and baskets. Marshes were agricultural benefits, and they led directly to the other benefits of the shore—the clams, oysters, lobsters, crabs, and fishes. There was a unity involved, a dependence of man on his environment, a living *with* it. Nowadays, this is a unity that would not seem particularly important except to those few who still live with it, or what is left of it. Urban money, very often from outside a community, is required for developments, recreation centers, factories, marinas, parking lots, shopping centers, and so on. The urgencies of population have become so extreme in some regions that a marsh is considered a luxury the community cannot afford. In others, a salt marsh is merely another potential section of land out of which development money can be made.

In many parts of the North Atlantic shore, marshes have been used as dumping grounds, with ghastly results. They are gray depositories of trash, sewage, and oily wastes. That this is not to our advantage may need little argument, but that it is our poverty to lose a salt marsh is a hard point to argue, and needs knowledge and authority behind it. A marsh is so rich in life, it involves so many intricate relationships, it nourishes the young of so many different species under so many different conditions of area and relative salinity, that adequate studies of it are only just beginning. It stands between land and sea, taking from both and giving to both, comprising a network of complex ecological strings that tie the unity of the ocean's edge together. The marsh acts as a great sponge, absorbing tremendous amounts of moisture, and as a protective buffer for the land against storm waves and flood tides.

In order to convince one another on its behalf, we keep reiterating the facts about a marsh's organic matter, its production in terms of so many tons an acre, a production as rich or richer than farm land in Iowa, its value as a spawning area for game fish such as striped bass and flounder, or for the shrimp that abound in its brackish estuaries. The tidal marsh, the tidal creek or estuary, the wide, flat, springy ground covered with tough grasses, the peat that is its foundation, are thus of measurable economic importance. At the same time, it may be said that we can live without shrimp, sea bass, flounder, or shellfish, those of us, at least, who are not directly involved with that kind of livelihood, and most of us are not. To argue that the destruction of salt marshes results in a tremendous loss of productive energy that may have serious effects on our economy is like repeating the statistics about how the number of trees and birds has decreased and how much topsoil has been lost. Four hundred thousand acres blow or wash away every year, but not necessarily my half acre or my city. If you are not enough interested in birds to count them, you can readily say that there are just as many now as there used to be; and the great number of trees merely proves how expendable they are.

Perhaps it is as an open and at the same time untouched and secret place, a matrix of variety, complex and wild, full of the new and renewing colors, changes and motions that we admire in all nature, that we have to defend a salt marsh, a place we can still go to to learn, to be enlightened. Its longevity is an asset we cannot match.

The great character of marshes lies in their wide and various use of the elements that invest them. They contain grasses whose roots are wet with salt water all the time; grasses and plants that are accustomed to occasional wetting or alternate flooding by the tides; grasses, sedges, and reeds that are adapted to being exposed to the sun, strong winds, and salt spray. If a salt marsh merges with a brackish and then a freshwater environment, the transitional zone may be wide and gradual enough to contain any number of life forms.

A marsh builds up by plant root systems. The waters that flow over it carry the materials and nutrient salts from plant decomposition to feed plankton in tidal estuaries, plankton that is eaten in turn by fish and shellfish. The nutrients from offshore waters are added to those of the marsh, and to its productivity. From the

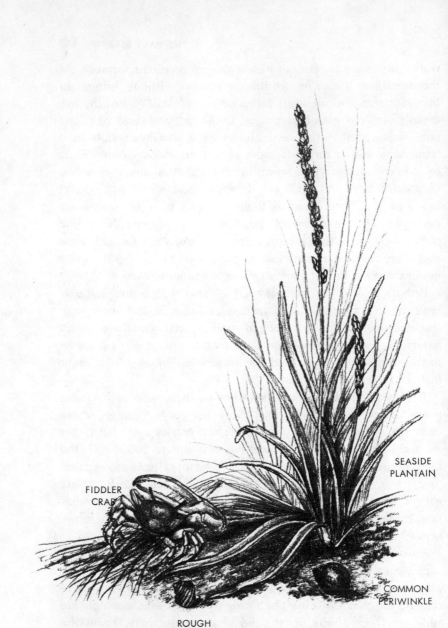

FIDDLER
CRAB

SEASIDE
PLANTAIN

ROUGH
PERIWINKLE

COMMON
PERIWINKLE

ribbed mussels and the periwinkles along the shore back to the jutting border of trees, a marsh may encompass any number of different communities, each dependent in its own fashion on the cycles of growth and decay, and on the fresh sea winds and waters that bathe them all.

A marsh is a unity and a series of unities. Vegetation begins a little below mean tide level, and from there back to inland woods there is a series of fairly definite zones, the outcome of differences in salinity and wetness. The peaty ledges and banks facing the open water, a spongy, slippery ground, are built and held together by the saltwater cordgrass or "thatch," with its tough, round stems and long, coarse, sharply pointed leaves. It can stand more wetness than most of the other marsh plants, and is found farthest out, but it will die if it is covered continually by salt water, as may happen when a bank slumps and falls into a tidal creek. Behind it, on levels reached only by high or unusually high tides, a different species of cordgrass predominates, smaller and with a more delicate texture, that makes a finer-textured peat. It has thinner, nearly grasslike leaves, grows in a characteristically matted fashion, and was the plant most harvested as salt hay.

Spikegrass is often mixed with the small cordgrass, and growing on the margins, at a somewhat higher and drier level, is a rush called black grass. In the salt marsh there may also be sections of salt-marsh bulrush, the chairmaker's rush, as well as two or three kinds of glasswort or samphire whose fleshy stems contain tasty salt juices. These are plants that tend to range from a little below high-tide levels to extreme high tides.

The upper part of a marsh, where the black grass grows as far back as those areas covered only by spring or storm tides, is often called a salt meadow, and here are flowering plants such as sea lavender, seaside aster, and seaside goldenrod. Blue-eyed grass may be found at intervals, and so may seaside gerardia, which has small pinkish-purple flowers. The salt meadow is sometimes rich

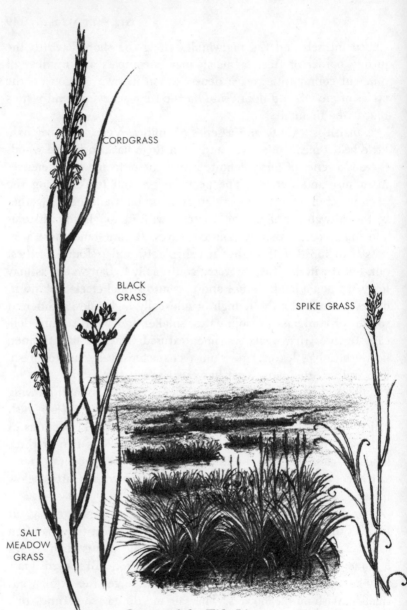

CORDGRASS

BLACK
GRASS

SPIKE GRASS

SALT
MEADOW
GRASS

**Grasses of the Tide Line**

with the yellow flowers of the goldenrod, interspersed with delicate lilac asters or the tiny, light-purple flowers of fleabane, smelling slightly of camphor; and it is the home of the orach, a plant with gray-green, trowel-shaped leaves, related to the pigweed of inland vegetable gardens.

Like the rest of the earth that is subject to changing seasons, marsh activity dies down and regenerates during the year. In May or June, for example, when saltwater cordgrass pokes its short spears through the peat along the shore, and alewives run into the estuaries, the cattails in brackish regions farther inland are stiff and neat, with perfect blades and crisp sheaths. The iris blooms; the leaves of the seaside goldenrod are plump and new. A song sparrow sings, bright and bold. A black duck, fifty feet in the air, circles around and around a marsh; and redwings are posted through the cattails that swing and flash in the wind and sunlight, at all points of the compass.

The cattails have flexible leaves and long root stalks spreading through the mud of the marsh, and as they grow they build a protective environment of their own. Muskrats feed on their rootstocks and tubers, and where cattails form islands that jut up above tide level, these islands become muskrat lodges, with entrances below the water. Ducks often nest among the cattails, as the redwings and grackles do. The weasel prowls through them on the hunt for meadow mice that feed on the hummocks or thread their way among the grasses, and mink search them for mice, frogs, and snakes. There are water snakes and black snakes in this community, and numbers of insects frequent it the year round.

Inland from the sea there are unceasing changes of color throughout the year. The black grass is the first to flower; its fruit turns brown quite early in the summer, so it is readily distinguished. The salt-marsh reeds and grasses are blue-green and yellow-green in the summer, red and tawny and gold in the fall,

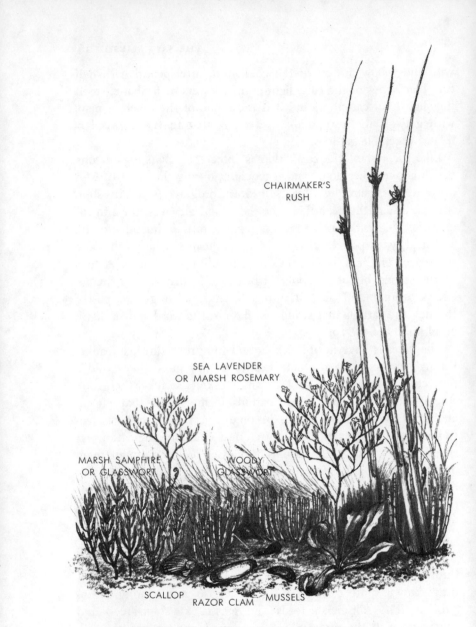

CHAIRMAKER'S
RUSH

SEA LAVENDER
OR MARSH ROSEMARY

MARSH SAMPHIRE
OR GLASSWORT

WOODY
GLASSWORT

SCALLOP

RAZOR CLAM

MUSSELS

Plants of the Salt Marsh, High Tide Line

dun-colored in winter. The flowers of salt-hay grass make violet patches on the marsh in midsummer. Spikegrass is still blue-green in September when the black grass has begun to die down. At the same time, the sea lavender or marsh rosemary is blooming —a bouquet in itself with light woody stems and a profusion of small, delicate, lavender-blue flowers. Another grass that keeps its color well into the fall is the giant reed or *Phragmites*, an extremely tall plant, reaching six or even eight feet, often growing in large stands that are spectacular when their plumes sway in the wind. But where it has supplanted cattails it does not serve the same function as a food provider for muskrats and wildfowl, or as cover for nesting birds.

All days are open over the salt marsh. Like a treeless plain, it is a place for the sky to enter. Its wide, seaward stretches with fiddler crabs, ribbed mussels, and snails, with gulls stalking, pools flicking with saltwater minnows, creeks with fingerling fish, are tidally oriented, ground that is neither beach nor dry land, but something in between—a moist region forever in wait for the next return or withdrawal of the sea. It is a refuge for migrants of the air, the ducks and geese. Rains slant over it unobstructed. Winter winds sweep stiffly across it. The sunset fires go out over long horizons. Light shafts penetrate enormous clouds overhead. And in the early autumn the winds blow full and loose over land and sea.

In the upper levels farther inland, the reeds, cattails, and tall grasses in their growing season are a multitude of shining leaves, and they sound with all the airs that come through them. This part of a marsh, from brackish back to fresh water, takes the puffs and roaring of the wind, and the reeds sway and swish, grasses touch together lightly, ticking and scraping, joined in the summer by the insistent rasping of crickets. At the margins of ditches and creeks, pickerel frogs jump at a man's approach, or there is a splash as a muskrat in a great hurry dives into a hole. Low-tide mud shows the tracks of coons, night herons, and spotted sandpipers. These bare, slick surfaces of mud along the banks of a tidal creek support an intricate community of diatoms, dinoflagellates, and various algae, food for insects, crustaceans, and birds, and also for those that will benefit when a proportion of it is washed into tidal waters. Some of these algae presumably become part of the plankton that feeds clams or oysters in an estuary.

Sparrows flit through the marsh at low levels, disappearing quickly and easily among its stalks and stems. Rails are also hard to see. The thin-bodied Virginia rail slides through the narrow spaces between the marsh grasses, so that it is not often seen, even when it flies up and disappears after being surprised. A bittern may start up with a squawk when you come upon it, but it is expertly camouflaged with striped, light-brown plumage that blends into the marsh vegetation, where it stands stiffly, its outline lost to the eye.

A spotted sandpiper feeds on the banks of a tidal creek when the mud is bare at low tide. It teeters, moving forward in short, sudden rushes, its bill exploring as it goes. The foraging bird travels along the bank, parallel with the water's edge, picking insects out of the algae which are spread across rusty-colored mud laden with "bog iron," then returns along a parallel course on a higher level, methodically working over the ground. Between forays, it drinks brackish water from the stream or makes a short flight to the opposite bank. A Wilson's snipe feeds in the same area, stolidly and deliberately, probing the mud at the water's edge with its long bill, pausing from time to time, but unlike the sandpiper staying in much the same place. Its light-tan head and back are strongly striped, making it hard to see in the marshes, and when surprised it flies up suddenly, with a harsh squeak or rasping note. At the same time a kingfisher may be poised in an overhanging swamp maple, from which it makes a slanting dive into the stream to catch a fish. An immature night heron or "quawk"

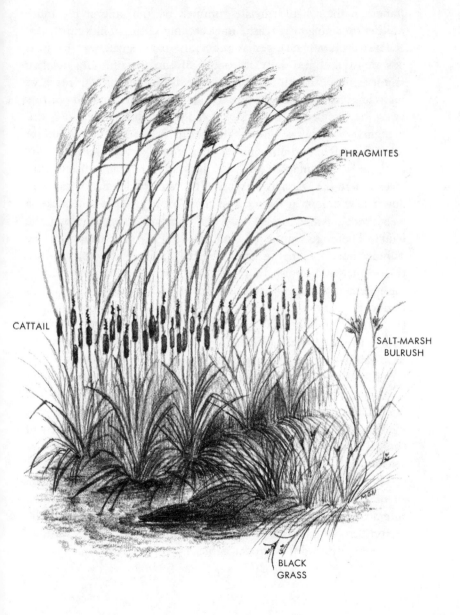

PHRAGMITES

CATTAIL

SALT-MARSH
BULRUSH

BLACK
GRASS

stands on these banks in late summer, pecking idly at the mud, waiting for a frog or crayfish, and catching nothing, flies upstream.

The vegetation changes as pure salt marsh gives way to areas less moist and less salty, through all the variations of relative salinity, from salt through brackish to fresh, beyond the reach of the tides. Near the highest tide seaside goldenrod is loaded with its heavy September bloom, thick deep-yellow heads standing and swinging. Switchgrass grows along the fringe of the marsh on somewhat higher ground and above it grow bayberry, beach plum, pitch pine, red maple, oak, and hickory. Along the marsh and creek where the water is increasingly fresh, the lobelia or cardinal flower may bloom in season, and there are arrowhead and pickerel weed; alder, willow, sweet gale, and buttonbush grow along the banks. There are clumps of mallows with big pink flowers in the summertime, and in the fresh streams that turn by degrees into tidal estuaries, tiny fish move like quick shadows, or hang vibrating together in suspended animation. A big snapping turtle, death to ducklings, swims down slowly when the tide comes in to deepen the stream, and there are painted and spotted turtles along the banks. In the stream's bends and quiet eddies, and up around its headwaters, are an increasing variety of freshwater fishes. Pickerel frogs begin to be replaced by green frogs and bullfrogs. Catbirds and northern yellowthroats supplant or join the herons and rails. The cattails, spearing sunward by the millions, sway in the light and the wind. Inland from them is poison ivy, bright red in the fall, and beech, maple, and oak trees, where the blue jays scream.

Through these and other scenes throughout the year, each life, small or large, simple or complex, takes part in the unending interaction of water, grasses, and mud, of tidal rhythms and the seasons' freezing and thawing. The marsh environment is wonderfully intricate, and it is irreplaceable.

# VISITORS FROM THE SEA

**8**

THE NORTH ATLANTIC SHORES, interlaced as they are with tidal creeks and estuaries, bordered by rocky coves or salt marshes binding the sea and the land, receive not only the wash and wreckage of the sea, the bottles and the planks, but many of its animals. Not that sea monsters are to be expected, but the actual visitors are fascinating enough. Some are strays from warmer waters, such as sea turtles; some fishes, such as the crevalle or jack, appear regularly off southern New England but rarely move into the Gulf of Maine. A small, bright-red fish known as the little big-eye, a native of the Caribbean and the Gulf of Mexico, appears during the summer on the southern side of Cape Cod, occasionally rounding it. Anyone picking up this brilliant little fish along a northern beach might be justified in thinking it had come from somebody's home aquarium.

You would not expect to see, off New England or Canada, the flying fish that are common to blue-green waters of tropical seas and the Gulf Stream; but they have been reported now and then over the years. The ocean sunfish also strays from warm waters beyond the continental slope and is reported in shallow waters along the coast. It may grow to ten feet in length. The head and foretrunk of its body are all of a piece, ending with two rear fins by which it propels itself, waving them from side to side. A weak swimmer at best, a sunfish astray in cold northern waters is reduced to helplessness, and soon dies. Certain species of sea turtles that also wander into the Gulf of Maine and the Labrador Current also succumb, especially during the winter months. The green turtle, a remarkable navigator, traveling 1,400 miles from the coast of Brazil to its breeding grounds on Ascension Island and back again, may appear off New England, though rarely north of Massachusetts. Leatherbacks, the largest of these turtles, are occasionally reported in New England waters during the summer. Others, like the loggerhead and the ridley, are often found dead along our winter shores. These two species are confirmed wanderers, having been reported in Scotland and the Scilly Isles off Cornwall, but like other sea turtles they cannot drift far from warm waters without danger. They swim from the south in the waters of the Gulf Stream, which have a fairly consistent temperature of around 70°F., but since they cannot survive in waters much below 50° F., they cannot safely range very far from the stream in northern latitudes, especially during the winter.

It is interesting to note that the Gulf Stream, from whose warm currents sea turtles may stray to their doom, was, conversely, of real benefit to sailors in the past. During the great sailing days of New England, many ships whose sails were "all frozen" and whose ropes were "like iron," as one captain put it on leaving New York Harbor in December, were able to thaw out as they traveled farther east into the Gulf Stream. But sea turtles, for all their direction-finding ability, and their power and agility as swimmers, are still more or less at the mercy of the ocean currents where they feed.

Harbor porpoises may also be found beached on northern shores after winter storms. A finback whale occasionally is stranded close to a beach, or comes in to shallow water because it is sick or dying. Schools of potheads or blackfish—not fish at all but whales—still chase food close to shore and into tidal streams. What causes whales to become stranded has long been a puzzle. Science has found one possible explanation in the working of a whale's sonar system. Like bats in the air, whales emit sounds that are echoed in their ocean medium. It is this endowment that permits them to find prey and to avoid obstacles. But on a very gently sloping ocean bottom, the increasing shallowness toward shore is so gradual that the whale's echolocation system does not detect marked changes, as it would if it were approaching a steep, rocky coast. As a result, the whale is trapped in the shallows, where it suffocates, no longer supported by the water, and unable to fill its lungs.

Colonists in Massachusetts began hunting whales in local waters as early as 1630. At first their whaling was confined to taking small whales, such as blackfish and humpbacks, that were found inshore; but as these became increasingly scarce, whaling ships were built to undertake longer voyages. The principal whale then sought in the North Atlantic was the right whale because its unusual buoyancy kept it afloat on the surface when killed, so that it was more readily handled for commercial purposes than whales of other species; it was the "right" whale to catch, thus its common name. The right whale furnished oil for soap, paint, and lamps, and baleen or whalebone for corsets and other things that needed strength and elasticity. The baleen, which takes the place of teeth in whales that feed on plankton, is a filtering device that grows down from the roof of the animal's mouth in the form of plates, smooth on the outside and fringed within. When a right whale feeds on shrimplike crustaceans or mollusks, it swims forward with its scooplike jaw extended, its mouth open, and the front of its head above water. When enough food has been filtered out of the water by the baleen plates, the animal dives underwater and swallows its catch.

The remains of a basking shark are still reported from time to time as indisputable evidence that the sea monster is more than a myth. This shark, which reaches tremendous size, sometimes a length of nearly sixty feet, is a mild animal that eats plankton, sifting it by means of its gill-rakers. Dead basking sharks decay quickly on shore. When their bodies have been reduced to very little but a backbone with bits of muscle and cartilaginous material sticking to it, the pile of remains gives to an imagination bent on discovering the sea monster just what it needs to work on. The basking shark got its name because of its habit of swimming about at the surface of the water with its mouth open, collecting plankton.

Hammerhead sharks, which lurk close to the bottom just offshore, do not belong in this harmless category, but have been known on occasion to attack swimmers. The first recorded attack by a shark in American waters was by a hammerhead off Long Island in 1815. This shark's name comes from two hammerlike appendages with eyes mounted at their ends on either side of its head. The resulting spread of the eyes undoubtedly permits a wider field of vision and better depth perception—advantages that would explain the evolution and survival of this odd structure. There is also a theory that the hammerhead achieves better balance because of these fleshy projections. Both theories may be correct. Since hammerheads feed primarily on other fishes, superior vision and maneuverability aid them greatly in obtaining their prey.

Aside from irregular marine visitors, or southern species straying from their normal range, there are some animals that are resident along a good deal of the North Atlantic coast but that are seen only at intervals, at any rate along its more southerly reaches. Notable among them are the seals. Those of the North Atlantic are hair seals, lacking the fine undercoat which gives fur seals their value. Nevertheless, harbor and harp seals, and the less common hooded and gray species—all of them hair seals—are still killed for their oil, and the very young animals are taken for their skins and pelts. The center of this pursuit is Newfoundland. The harbor seal, ranging southward to North Carolina, and breeding between southern New England and the Arctic, is fairly common during the summer along areas such as the islanded coast of Maine. It is rarely found far offshore, since it cannot sleep for long periods in open water, but must return to land each night. As soon as the young, born in the spring, are able to accompany their mothers, they head for estuaries, following alewives and other fishes that make spring spawning runs into fresh water.

Harbor seals are a great deal less numerous than they used to be. As fish eaters they have endured much random persecution; there have been bounties on them in many states, though in Massachusetts the bounty was removed recently. Along the Labrador coast and in the Arctic, the harbor seal has some economic value as a supplier of meat and blubber for men and dogs and of skins for making garments. In most other areas it is the fisherman's enemy, damaging his salmon and herring nets and acting as a carrier of the "codworm." This is a parasitic worm which during its immature stages occurs in the flesh of cod and other species of fish; though it is relatively harmless, it renders the fish less marketable.

But in fact it appears to be the harp seal, backbone of the sealing industry from Newfoundland north, that is the preferred host of the codworm.

The gray seal, whose North Atlantic population, widely scattered off the shores of eastern Canada, now numbers 5,000 at most, probably occurred at one time as far south as Cape Cod, Nantucket, and Block Island. A tiny remnant herd, most recently estimated to number fifteen, was discovered breeding on sandspits off Nantucket by an alert fisherman not satisfied with their local identification as harbor seals. In color the two species appear much the same when wet, but the snout of the gray seal, especially in older males, becomes considerably elongated and rounded, giving rise to the name "horsehead," whereas the harbor seal's muzzle is short.

In Newfoundland the sealing industry was once second only to that of the cod. Fleets of spring sealers set off the end of March to return with nearly 10,000 pelts. Thousands of men were involved in a pursuit that was a peril for seals and hunters alike. The great danger to the hunter, who trailed his quarry on foot over shifting ice floes, was being stranded away from the ship. Hundreds of men died that way. Since prime sealskin is still in demand, especially for skiing jackets, and brings a high price—the Hudson's Bay Company used to get five dollars for pelts, but the price has now gone up to thirty-five dollars—the hunt continues, though the number of men involved has declined from 10,000 to 2,000. The harp seal has greatly declined in numbers. The population of harp seals, numbering 3,000,000 as recently as 1951, had been reduced to some 1,250,000 by 1960, and unless strong conservation measures are taken, it may not be many years before the industry is obliged to shut down altogether.

Such marine visitors as sharks, whales, and seals—and even the Portuguese man-of-war that may drift from the Gulf Stream into the shallow waters of southern New England—are occasional for

the most part. But fishes of one kind or another—whether they are seasonal migrants such as the salmon or shad that comes each year to inland waterways, or whether, like the haddock, they are caught off the coast during the winter, or whether they are salt-water minnows and sticklebacks living in the estuaries—are with us the year around. Seen or unseen, they are omnipresent, inshore and beyond the coastline.

Just as the birds migrate from shore to shore, and the water itself moves in and out, so the fishes thread the waters of the coast in all its turnings. Under the trills, laughs, and mutterings of gulls and terns, they wheel and run in the shallows, moving into tidal inlets from deep water and out again. They migrate for unknown distances over the continental shelf. They scavenge around a rock or a wharf. They sink into the sand, or hover in the channels that cut through a tidal marsh. The story of their abundance is still to be told.

Mackerel, whitefish, halibut, flounder, smelt, butterfish, tuna—the names of marketable fishes known to most coastal Americans, and others far inland and across the seas, do not mean as much to us as they did once. Processed fish food, either as frozen fillets or concentrated into bricks to stave off famine, is not the same thing as the strong-smelling, slick-sided catch which meant a family or a village could survive a winter. Fish, of course, were basic to the founding of the New World. A cod or a herring which was one of a community's few articles of commerce, its produce for export, seems a great deal more, simply as a physical object, than it does in a nation whose food commodities are legion.

Small local trawlers that rock through winter waves along the coast remind us of a cold and ancient trade. European factory ships and their attendant vessels ply the Grand Banks or Georges Bank, arousing apprehension, and pointing to the diminished state of our own fishing fleets. More millions are being spent on fiber-glass fishing boats for sportsmen than on our professional ships, but that there are still fishing fleets from a number of nations is proof that the fish are still there, at least for a while. It is conceivable, though hard to prove, that some important species are on the decline. The riches of the sea are commensurate with its vastness, and it is often said that they have hardly begun to be exploited. The reproduction of fishes is adjusted to this vastness and the omnivorous world they live in. A good-sized female cod will lay several million eggs. As their technological means keep improving so does the intensity with which men fish. The sea still implies an overproduction in its own right, but the human race is doing its best to cut it down, whether this is to our ultimate advantage.

Now and then, those of us on shore who cannot have the privilege of seeing the reality being hauled out of green depths and thrown on the decks may glimpse original abundance, and even some of our earlier ways of taking advantage of it. On the coast of Newfoundland or the outer coast of Labrador, in June and July, it is possible to witness the spawning of the capelin in fantastic numbers along the shore. The capelin is a small fish resembling a smelt. Its range is in the high seas of the Arctic and sub-Arctic, and it is a basic food of whales and cod. In the spawning season, shoals of capelin school in the shallow waters, the massed lines of their green-backed bodies looking like beds of eelgrass. Hundreds of kittiwakes, graceful little seagulls, fly over them, constantly dipping, turning, and diving, in circular, whirling snow squalls of activity. When the capelin spawn, they "roll" in on the tide along the gravelly and pebbly shoreline and are often stranded on the beaches and die lodged between the rocks. Foot-deep windrows of their sticky, reddish eggs lie on rocky beaches, and the capelin themselves, their silvery bodies caught between the rocks, are shoveled up by the ton to be used for fish meal. Fresh capelin are also eaten locally.

When these multitudes of fish are running offshore, swarming dense as bees and ruffling the surface of the water, they attract not only sea birds but the cod, the great predator of North Atlantic waters. Along the shore the great waves wash in, cold and slow, over the rocks. The wind fans the sea surface with spreading, shifting patches, silvery dark. White, rafted companies of gulls ride on the water. They drift and dive where the capelin are running, and the heavy-bodied codfish jump straight up, plunge over, fall back into the water. Sometimes fishermen gig for these great fish in the time-honored way, piling the big, dark, slippery cod into their white dories hour after hour, even as a new moon begins to appear and redness deepens behind the mountains.

Farther south, along the coast of Nova Scotia, are the northern limits of the alewife or freshwater herring, known variously in Canada as "gaspereau," "herring," or "kyak," according to the locality. Of the two species, which are hard to tell apart, one, *Alosa pseudoharengus*, is called the blackback, and the other, *Alosa aestivalis*, is called the blueback or glut herring. The blackbacks start up numerous streams and rivers to spawn, as do the bluebacks, but they do not usually reach the lakes and ponds at the heads of streams; they stop in waters closer to the sea. Alewives are not so numerous as they used to be, nor so much in demand, although they are commercially exploited in their more plentiful runs as cat food or as pickled herring, and today are even salted and smoked on occasion. Their spawning habits, which bring schools of them back to what are believed to be the freshwater systems where they grew up—in the manner of the Atlantic salmon—announce them in the spring.

As early as the beginning of May, they begin to migrate through narrow channels between dark-green islands to enter the rocky streams of Nova Scotia. Here are old areas of subsistence farming, where gray knotty shingles slip year by year from venerable barns with manure piled against their foundations, and stacks of cordwood alongside. Very rarely, you may see a man with oxen hitched to a wooden plow. Here and there along the shore are drying racks for fish, although these are used to a greater extent in Newfoundland and the Gaspé. Where the alewives enter from the sea the gulls mob a narrow inlet, channel, or stream, screaming, chasing each other, catching the foot-long fish and dropping them on the rocks. In some towns young boys come with boxes and pails, and with long-handled dip nets to scoop up the fish as they crowd a narrow inlet—the spring advent which used to be celebrated from Nova Scotia to the Carolinas.

These fish swim inland progressively later as the latitude from south to north increases, a few at first followed by the major runs several weeks later. Thus, alewives may be expected in quantity around the twenty-fifth of April on the north side of Cape Cod, and about the tenth of May at Damariscotta, Maine, where a broad tidal river is met by a small rocky stream with man-made stone terraces and resting pools to help the alewives in their ascent. Alewives crowding a stream, leaping against the current to link sea and land, arrive in deep, shadowy, sinewy processions out of tidal waters. They climb the frothing torrents, vibrantly, persistently. The reproductive power of the sea is in them, a relentless drive that carries with it a risk, a precarious balance. They lift up and on through the water until they reach a quiet pond, taken by the thousands on their way—a lift which is part of depth and range, and the perpetuation of a race.

Shad and salmon are also anadromous fish, growing up in salt water and spawning in fresh. They have been vastly reduced in numbers since colonial days because of this vulnerable inland migration. The building of dams and other obstructions, the pollution of rivers and streams, and in recent years the excessive use of pesticides over wide areas, have had a cruel effect on their population. Most of our major rivers along the more populated parts of the coast have not had any salmon runs for at least a century.

The Atlantic eel practices a salmonlike migration, but in the reverse direction, being a catadromous fish that spends its adult life in freshwater streams, rivers, and estuaries and then returns to salt water to breed. After wriggling in as little elvers, it is believed that most of the females, which grow larger than the males, go far inland along the streams and rivers, whereas the male eels more often stay in coastal areas such as marshes and bays. Years later, at sexual maturity, both move downstream and out into salt water for the start of their spawning journey. Where they spawned was a mystery until 1925, when a Danish marine biologist, Johannes Schmidt, traveled thousands of miles across the North Atlantic, taking samples and plotting the distribution of ever smaller eel larvae, until he traced them to a general spawning area in the Sargasso Sea, south of Bermuda. Adult eels spawn deep in the ocean and then die. The eggs float in the sea, eventually hatching into transparent larvae that drift with the ocean currents. Some of their millions drift toward Europe, and the others toward America, carried for about a year by the waters of the Gulf Stream. These flat, leaflike "glass eels" change into narrow, rounded, grayish-black elvers when they reach the coast, and after this metamorphosis they begin to swim against the current and to show a preference for a freshwater or brackish instead of a saltwater environment, entering streams, rivers, and waterways of every sort. The European eels are somewhat slower than the American to metamorphose from larva to elver, and they continue to drift with the plankton in the sea until they reach Europe, where the same process takes place. There is evidently a genetic difference between the two species in both their orientation to the land and the timing of their responses—a difference so infallible that no European eels have been found entering American rivers, nor have American eels been recorded in Europe.

For most of us, fish are not of the bone and marrow of the people that they still are in some Canadian communities, and that they were in New England not many years ago—even though men now go after them with greater intensity than they did, and study

**Alewives Entering Run**

them literally in depth. The fishing industry now calls on science where once it was completely at the mercy of the fish—especially of those that periodically disappear. This is still the way of the sea herring, which are taken close to shore along the Bay of Fundy and in Maine, rather than far offshore as in Europe. In these places the interest has been mainly in juvenile fish packed as sardines, though adults are also processed for oil, fish meal, and cat food. They are chased and preyed upon by cod, striped bass, and the ferocious bluefish, by tuna, salmon, mackerel, dogfish, haddock, and hake; and they are eaten in great quantity by finback whales. Very young herring are a favorite food of squid. For all its awe-inspiring abundance, the herring supply has a way of fluctuating locally from year to year and from season to season. One year it is a glut on the market, bringing prices drastically down; in another, its failure to appear may bring a shutdown of sardine canneries.

Herring are prolific spawners; off one part or another of this continent some of them are laying eggs during nearly every month of the year. Along the Atlantic coast, spawning reaches a peak in spring and again in the fall. Local fisheries are able to make a catch of the adult herring when they have been present offshore during the spawning seasons or the winter months; but the herring cannot be counted on to appear, since they may quite suddenly change their habits or migratory routes. The sardine fisheries depend on the spring and summer schooling of young herring three or four inches long, not far from shore, where they are trapped with weirs or, more often, with stop seines enclosing an area where schools have been located, sometimes with the help of spotter planes.

The essential problem in a study of Atlantic herring is to find out how many fish are out there in the deep, circulating waters, and where they are likely to come from when they appear—if they appear. Which sounds like a nearly impossible assignment to begin with. If the fish do not show themselves, where can they be? The fishing depends on these young herring to come in to local coves and bays; if they do not, what may have happened to keep them offshore? The answer involves a study in detail of the waters of the inshore environment. The little herring have other problems beside predators. Research is concerned with the spawning location of the herring, and also what happens to eggs and young. The herring lay their eggs on gravelly or rocky bottoms, ranging from a few fathoms to as much as thirty fathoms below the surface. When the young hatch they drift with the current. In fact, those hatched in the spawning area of Georges Bank, along with many other species of fish, may drift beyond the continental shelf and fail to survive, passing the threshold of temperature change which they can tolerate. Wind conditions affect the normal circulation of the waters and carry them far off course. Sometimes severe storms drive the young fish up to die on the beaches, or they may be infected with disease organisms. Only a tiny percentage of the potential number of herring survive. Nevertheless, their general abundance shows no decline; which says a great deal about the fecundity of Atlantic waters, as well as of the herring themselves.

Among schooling alewives or herring and their deep-sea relative the mackerel—whose disappearances can be even more dramatic —there is a dimension all but unimaginable to man, an alliance with distances, depths, currents, turbulences, an easy flowing of response built into them by instinct, a quick sensitivity. Fish are an embodiment of abundance. It is in their nature, and in the nature of their environment; it is a necessity for their survival.

It is quite possible that the alewives belong to local offshore stocks, which may be genetically distinguished from each other. This could partly account for their evident ability to return to the stream in which they grew up, even if they were only an inch or two in length when they left it. When they are at sea, in other words, a distinct, local race of alewives may school miles offshore but always in a certain relation to its home base. It is also possible that spawning populations of sea herring can be biologically distinguished from each other, both onshore and offshore—those of the coast of Maine from those of Nova Scotia, or of Georges Bank; and, if so, their orientation would have nothing to do with the freshwater systems of the land but with an environment exclusively marine. Studies have indicated the possibility, but the evidence is by no means conclusive. It may be that any species of fish, however far its population may roam, is somehow oriented to familiar sea surroundings, perhaps sometimes to land connections, too, but perhaps more often not. Such is the world of the sea, in which spiny dogfish on annual migrations from Virginia to Labrador, or a salmon wandering hundreds of miles from the river where it was spawned, knows in some way where it is. A fish may perhaps lose its way, but it may also be sensitive to clues, as it may be that birds are on their migrations. It is worth noting, too, that the floors of the sea undergo relatively little alteration over long periods of time; that seasonal temperatures and the direction of the currents are much the same from year to year in any given offshore region, in spite of major interruptions and changes analogous to the storms and natural upheavals we know on land.

In the relatively cold waters of the North Atlantic coastal range, we know that fish are variously sensitive to temperature. Alewives come inland in early spring when the fresh water issuing into the sea becomes warmer, if only by a few degrees. Herring have been observed to swim sluggishly when Bay of Fundy waters were at their coldest in late winter, and to become more active again when the water warmed to temperatures of forty to forty-three degrees. Sudden freezing in shallow waters can kill off large numbers of local shore fishes, such as the cunner or sea perch. Some fishes prefer relatively warm waters and others prefer them cool. That cold-water fish, the cod, for example, is found in northern latitudes during summer and fall, journeying south of New England only during the winter and early spring. It spawns over the shoal waters of Georges Bank in February, March, and April. The bluefish, armed with a jaw full of formidable needle-sharp teeth, prefers a warmer environment, and appears off southern New England only during the summer. The flounders or flatfishes show a great range of adaptation to heat and cold, as well as to all kinds of bottom habitat in both deep and shallow waters.

Differences in temperature mean different movements at sea. Some travelers escape extreme temperatures during winter months by moving southward, or into deeper waters over the continental shelf. Others, which might be called local residents since they live in shallow tidal waters and estuaries, go into a state of sluggishness and inactivity during the winter. The common mummichog or salt-water minnow, which lives in tidal creeks, pools, and ditches, buries itself in the mud when the weather is coldest.

Every cubic yard of water along the North Atlantic coast is or has been traveled by fishes of all kinds, shapes, and sizes, and every variety of bottom ground is inhabited by them. Ranging from fresh to brackish to salt, and with gradations in salinity that increase in the forbidding depths beyond the shelf, there are many possible ranges of existence. Fish feed on plankton, on each other, on sea worms or mollusks, on waste and seaweed and living tissue, each being an exceptional form of that use in a vast environment. A fish may not be endowed with much intelligence, but it is eloquent in itself of its world, a sea pitiless and full of greed, with its sharks and bluefish, its endless fragile lives, beautiful as the fusiform, rippled, and iridescent body of a mackerel, or grotesquely extravagant as a sculpin or a toadfish, wonderful in its providing, its storm of plankton innumerable as snowflakes, its living and multiplying clouds of roe.

Out from the shore the marine frontier still remains before us, whether as fishermen or as explorers. You can only guess what schools of fish may run under those rocking green waves where the cold salt smell surrounds you—except on the occasion when you see them as you do the capelin, covering the surfaces, or schools of bass or mackerel making slicks on the water to reveal themselves. When they come in as the alewives do in the spring, it is as if the sea had released some of its secrets for a time. Marine animals with silvery sides, they look too big for some of the ponds they enter, where white circles of cleared sand show sunfish nests on the bottom. They go forward insistently, upcurrent, their big eyes staring. When gulls or men mob or net them they wheel wildly, sometimes with a confused stampeding when pressed from behind. The special rhythm of their schooling and its mysterious direction can belong only to the sea. They are of the depths, made to school in great numbers, to escape and survive by virtue of those numbers, to react swiftly, immediately. They have in them the purpose of the sea, the continual replenishment of its lives; but they have also, as particular fish, the ability to find their way, to smell and see, to feel all the pressures and changes in the water that surround them, to put exceptional energies to use.

# BIRDS AND THE WEATHER

**9**

THE WEATHER ON THE NORTHEAST COAST is known for its instability. There may be periods when cold drizzle or summer heat hangs on for many days, but for the most part change is the rule, day by day within the order of the seasons. The major air masses, tropical and polar, maritime or continental, changing in terms of the regions over which they move, meet, have marginal conflicts, and replace each other. Change and uncertainty seem to be continual; we

175

count on them for our daily greetings. There are parts of the world where the natives take the weather for granted, and hardly ever speak of it except as it has a direct bearing on the rice crop or hunting an antelope. Perhaps idle chatter about the weather is the habit of a civilization insulated against it, but the northeast weather is rough enough to justify any amount of talk.

The coastal climate also varies from section to section. The sea provides a generally moderating influence, since it has the capacity to store a vast amount of heat in its depths and so takes more time than the land to cool in the fall and to warm again in the spring. Shallow-water temperatures, however, vary considerably, and sudden changes occur which may be disastrous for marine animals. On the whole, the maritime process of warming and cooling is gradual and consistent compared with that of the land; on the open sea the range of temperature between summer and winter is fairly narrow. The water temperatures become gradually lower with the higher latitudes; and this has an effect not only on fish but on the local, coastal climate along the sea, where men complain and birds endure. We can assess the atmospheric conditions that influence us, and predict tomorrow to some extent; but the birds, and other animals, are equipped to meet it as it comes.

Changes in a single day can be extreme, especially along the New England coast, the "temperate" sector between north and south. On a February morning during the hours between a temporary receding of cold polar air and the intrusion of a new low-pressure system, with rain and warmer temperatures from the south and southwest, the sun shines brightly. It almost feels like spring, and resident chickadees respond with cheerful calls to light and warmth. Then clouds begin to roll in gray masses over the horizon as the day wears on. The wind freshens along the shore. By late afternoon the sun's pale disk diffuses yellow, pink, and green light through a smoky overcast. Pack ice that has collected along the shore for weeks now breaks; chunks of it are jostled by the surf, and there is a sound of heavy lapping where they float offshore. Snow or snowy ice covers the rocks, lies over a marsh behind the shoreline, and shoulders the banks of tidal creeks.

There is less wind and turbulence in the trees, the slopes and hollows above the shore, where chickadees are calling. The air sweeps in over a relatively bare landscape of water, beach, and marsh, hitting bluffs, outlying points, and low headlands, rounding corners with speed, slowing up behind them, but free to ride. Small flocks of meadowlarks fly inland across the marsh, or stop in the grasses, heads and sharp beaks pointing up, their tail feathers twitching, alert, nervous; and they fly with alternate quick wingbeats and glides. Occasional flickers pass overhead. In flight they have a slight resemblance to meadowlarks, but with a characteristic bound, and their tails are more angular.

Black ducks quack around a bend in the tidal stream, and then fly up into the wind in separate flocks. They veer and turn, dark wings with silvery undersides beating fast, wild, and wary. They change direction in flight, rising up in small numbers at alternating times, as if they were obeying all points of the compass. In contrast to their rising up, their high turning in the wind and beating down the shore, a kingfisher, with a rattling cry, wings in a direct low line across the marsh. Along the shore one dunlin and one sanderling, the remnants of big summer flocks in the area, feed intermittently along the narrow rim of the shore and then flit away. A flock of horned larks comes in to peck over the litter at the water's edge, and flies on again to a higher level, with an interrelated dipping and rising.

Tall-necked Canada geese ride offshore on the gray waters. Some of them have flocked on board a large ice cake that is gradually drifting out to sea. Big black-backed gulls, known to some as "ministers," stand on snowy rocks with herring gulls, growling throatily from time to time; many more gulls are on the water together, facing into the wind. Over the marsh and down the shore a big, gray, rough-legged hawk wheels majestically, high above all the other birds, and then sails away.

These few species of birds are here on the flat, open reaches of the shore for the food it affords, just as the chickadees work round a tree for insect eggs and larvae in its bark; but they are also here because of the weather. The wind bites and whines, moves from a moderate breath to a full roar, and they are of it. A storm arrives and passes. The continental, the polar, and the maritime airs meet, deploy, and shift their colossal forces, and the birds join this great movement in various motions of their own. For them it is complete and essential exposure, successful perhaps, as the terms may be applied to evolutionary adaptation, if not in terms of hazards. Birds are short-lived. The duck may die of cold or hunger when confined to a marsh in a northeast storm. Snow and ice can cover a food supply for birds that do not ordinarily winter in a moderate coastal area, and they may starve. The insulation of feathers and accumulated fat will not save them from the extremes of cold and a low food supply. Theirs is a harsh world as well as a fecund one. Of the birds, their quickness, their movements from place to place, their wide range as creatures of the air, it may be said that they belong to the weather.

Birds display a fittingness with respect to their environment, but not in the static sense of a shellfish lodged in a small area of sand, or a sculpin spending a lifetime in the vicinity of one rock. They carry their fittingness with them. They add to the sum of the place. Their motions, their physical equipment, may be attuned to the uses of a shore habitat, a mountain or a field, but not so as to bind them there. They belong in the wide context of such environments, and use the kind that is appropriate to them, and available. The migratory journeys of the birds seen along the shore on a February day are not all north to south in their orientation, but vary a great deal in latitude and direction. The rough-legged hawk frequents salt marshes and sandy coastlines with grassy areas, for the mice and shrews it finds there, and will start to migrate north when the snow melts. Horned larks migrate in late winter to the northern tundra, but meadowlarks may move only to fields farther inland. A large number of the black ducks common on Cape Cod nest in Newfoundland. A resident chickadee moves in the spring from winter feeding grounds to a nesting area perhaps only half a mile away; but there are terns and plovers that make a south-to-north migration halfway round the world. The white-winged scoter that winters offshore breeds in the marshes of central Canada and will fly there in the spring, moving from east to west over the Great Lakes.

The winter whereabouts of most birds of the open shore is uncertain. They will come back to winter in more or less the same place, year after year, depending on the species, but the location is less fixed than in the breeding season. Winter is often a time for wandering, when birds may travel very far from their breeding territories. How does a bird find its way back from great distances over the open sea or continental territories, across mazes of rivers, hills, and plains? Some of the flights are spectacular. A Manx shearwater was taken from its nesting burrow on the Welsh island of Skokholm several years ago, banded for identification, and flown to Boston. There it was released; and thirteen days later it arrived back at its burrow in Skokholm, having flown over 3,000 miles of ocean where no landmarks exist. Recent experiments indicate that some species of birds with regular wintering areas have similar skill in finding these after being released in completely unknown territory thousands of miles distant.

For all the migratory birds that find their way, a great many others seem to get lost. Accuracy may be combined with the tendency to be confused. Birds are frequently swept in directions they never aimed for, though they may be capable of going back and recovering their orientation. Science looks for reasons for migration as well as the homing ability, and finds many possibilities, such as the seasonal lengthening of daylight, which has an effect on the sex glands of birds, accounting for the migratory impulse to begin with, if not the orientation. During migration, birds may be able to find their direction by landmarks, by the moon or the sun, or even by constellations on clear nights. It is a fascinating subject, no less so because the solution may lie in the whole, rather than in any one of the parts, the whole life of a bird and its hereditary responses, millions on millions of years in the making, to its surroundings.

So this overhead restlessness and wandering, together with a specific predilection for some wood or shore, a food-gathering area to which beak and claw are fitted, is tied to the motions of the wind, and to changes in the light. The bird is a compass in itself, veering off course and returning, intrinsically oriented to the earth.

Birds have a fluid connection with environment and weather, as the horned larks flocking over chosen ground, landing together to feed, then rising again, have with one another. The single wanderer such as the rough-legged hawk, which frequents the same places, has its own way of riding the weather and exploring with it. Terns about to migrate in the fall gather on sandbars and feed in nearby waters, diving, dipping, crying harshly, a mutual tension in the quick, strong beat of their wings. When they fly off some September or October day for the south, they seem to go in a cool and glittering season that especially suits them.

Whatever impels birds to migrate in spring and fall, there is no specific correlation or timing that we can see. In the fall they often leave when the weather is still mild and food plentiful, before there seems to be a reason to leave. Shore birds collect and start to migrate in August before the summer is over. Spring migrations start northward from tropical regions where climate and weather are relatively constant. In order to reach a specific territory within a narrow range of days, as the redwings or swallows do, migratory birds must have an inner impulse to go at a time best suited to them; though in a general way the seasons, temperatures, changes in light, and other rhythms of environment maintain a consistency over the years, in spite of annual variations. You can predict

Horned Lark

the arrival of fish, the singing of spring peepers, the calls of the first redwings, just as you predict the spring.

Even if no causal connection between weather and migration can be proved, the weather may be a stimulus, setting off an impulse and timing which are already there. And, of course, weather itself, the movement of air masses and storms, plays a direct part in their passage. Birds may be triggered into migration by barometric pressure and other meteorological signs, but they have no built-in weather forecasting system—as some people believe—that allows them to anticipate storms or moving fronts. Most birds are precise in the times of their arrival after migration flights; but some "weather migrants"—the robin being a good example, which is among the first birds of spring—are delayed or spurred on by weather to an extent that the time of their arrival may vary from two to three weeks.

There are observations by W. H. Drury, research director of the Massachusetts Audubon Society, to show that wintering flocks of tree sparrows, which arrive in eastern Massachusetts in late October or early November, pause first in lowlands and river valleys, not moving to higher grounds until the cold weather deepens in December. With each storm during the winter, feeding flocks of these sparrows become increasingly restless, sometimes moving five or ten miles away. In February, when the days grow longer, small distinct groups of them start to break up and mix, and in mid-March the birds begin to sing and chase each other in anticipation of the courtship and mating challenges to follow, feeding until much later in the evening; and finally they disperse entirely from the wintering grounds, though not yet very far. They arrive at their breeding grounds in Labrador around the middle of May, after a journey of three or four days. Temperature and weather data suggest that an internal physiological timing mechanism prepares tree sparrows to disperse at some time after the tenth of March, and that this is set off by temperatures rising above forty-five degrees, especially by jumps of ten to fifteen degrees in one day. Temperature rises accompanied by storms do not impel the birds to depart but do make them sensitive to less strong stimuli in the following week.

These mid-March movements of sparrows, at the crucial time of year when the winter begins to break up, are simultaneous with other migrations. There are installations at South Truro, Massachusetts, where the coming and going of birds have been observed on a radar screen, though they are not easy to identify as to species. Several birds might make up one of a number of unidentified spots, referred to as "angels." The larger, slower-moving spots are probably herring gulls; fast-moving ones are likely to be shore birds such as sandpipers and plovers; and small, faint ones coming and going on the screen are identified as songbirds.

The radar showed that the dispersal of tree sparrows coincided with the first arrival of small songbirds in moderate numbers. This is the time when such other species as redwings, cowbirds, and grackles come to occupy the same ground. Then bluebirds, tree swallows, robins, and phoebes begin to arrive and sing in the stronger light, while the horned lark, the Canada goose, and the black duck are moving northward. Cold fronts with freezing rain or snow often hold up the early migrants, forcing them to gather in flocks and feed where they can. Indeed, the radar showed clear movements in reverse during such weather conditions. For insect-eating birds that have advanced northward too rapidly in the spring, outdistancing their food supply, the only hope of surviving may be to reverse direction and fly southward at once. The radar screen has shown that this is exactly what happens, thus accounting for reports nearly every year of "bewildered" birds migrating in the wrong direction. During one night after a cold front had passed on Cape Cod, for example, the northeasterly flight of birds was replaced by a milling movement, which was followed within only two hours by a mass flight toward the south.

In April, air masses that might normally start birds on a gradual northerly migration may force them far off course. While they are flying in a favorable wind, part of a tropical air mass from the Gulf of Mexico, a cold air mass from the western plains may press southeastward and push the whole warm system out to sea, with the result that the birds are forced out over the water, while a cold front stands as a barrier between them and the mainland. When that happens, these migrants fly over the sea for as long as their strength holds out. Given enough endurance, they may land on Cape Cod, in Maine, or Nova Scotia. Hence the arrival on this coast of some kinds of birds that would not normally appear for another month, as well as rarities such as the indigo bunting or summer tanager that should not be here at all.

Ornithologists long believed that birds migrating from inland flew toward the coast, and then followed it southward or northward. But Dr. Drury's radar investigations have shown that in reality only a few birds turn to follow the coastline, whereas the rest pour across it without changing course. It appears, in fact, that anywhere from ten to fifty times as many small birds migrate inland as along the coast.

If changes in the weather do not necessarily have any direct, causal connection with migration, they are simultaneous with it, and determine whether birds will begin to migrate or not. On spring days when the air is warm and the winds are favorable, birds move northward. In the fall they move southward after a period of rain followed by clear cold weather. They move with the seasons; their restlessness is the restlessness of the changing year.

Even where houses are thicker than trees, birds still come and go, many of them to remote places on another continent. To be a bird watcher is to extend your weather, and your range.

# BIRDS OF THE SEA

## 10

OVER COASTAL WATERS in the autumn months there are many kinds of birds on the move, migrants from breeding sites as far north as Labrador and Greenland. Sharp flashes of spray show gannets diving for fish from fifty to a hundred feet over the sea. Surf scoters ride the waves with ease and buoyancy. Flocks of double-crested cormorants travel by in slow heavy flights. As fall deepens, the common eiders arrive in increasing numbers from the north, long lines of them shuttling back and forth over offshore waters. Members of the family known as auks or alcids come down from their northern territories: dovekies, murres, an occasional razor-billed auk. Before the flightless great auk became extinct, it, too, used to undertake considerable migrations, traveling at least as far as Massachusetts, where its bones have been found.

In the United States, from Maine northward, the breeding islands of some of these, and of others such as the black guillemot (another alcid) and the petrels, are small islands that are surrounded by surf, whose native timothy grass, mustard, yarrow, pigweed, nettles, and briars grow rich on the nitrogenous droppings of generation after generation of birds. Farther north in Maritime Canada are high-cliffed headlands and rocky islands out in the sea, dark and dramatic outposts for many thousands of breeding pairs.

The great sea-bird colonies of the North Atlantic coast were among the first wildlife resources to be exploited by early fishermen and explorers. Of all the offshore islands on which these species nested, the most noted was flat-topped Funk Island off Newfoundland, of which Jacques Cartier declared that the birds were so plentiful "as to be incredible unless one has seen them." Most of the birds were gannets or members of the auk family. It was reported that when a sailor landed on the shore he must quickly obtain a good foothold or else the birds would rise in such numbers as to knock him over. Not all the birds, however, took wing when disturbed. One of them, the great auk, a large penguin-like black-and-white bird, "so fat it is marvelous," could not fly. In the ages during which it had lived on offshore Atlantic islands, it had been safe from mammalian predators—including the Indians, who feared to navigate the choppy seas. It had grown specialized, losing its powers of flight but developing a superior ability to pursue fish through water, using stubby wings as paddles.

In primeval America the great auk was abundant principally on Funk Island and three others off the coast of Iceland, but it was found also in the Canadian north; and in 1603 Gosnold found it nesting in the vicinity of Cape Cod, probably on Monomoy or Point Gammon. This unfortunate bird was awkward and ungainly on land, and since it was flightless it was unable to nest on the more protected upper rocks, with the result that with little effort it could be approached and clubbed to death. The first record of depredations upon it is a logbook notation from the Cartier ex-

**Kittiwakes Nesting**

pedition of 1534: each ship took about half an hour to salt down some five casks of great auks to be used as food on the homeward voyage. In a few more years sailors learned to capture this abundant source of meat with fences of stretched sailcloth with which they swept the docile birds toward a ship and into its hold.

The relative inaccessibility of the chief breeding islands of the great auk only deferred its complete extinction. By 1785 what remained of the birds on Funk Island was being killed with no thought that this immense colony could ever be destroyed. Crews spent the entire summer on the island, killing birds for feathers and oil. To obtain the latter, the carcasses were boiled in huge vats, and the fires themselves were wantonly stoked with still other carcasses. Even John James Audubon was convinced in the 1830s that vast numbers populated other islands off Newfoundland, but no such islands were ever found. It is believed that the last auk disappeared from continental North American shores about the time Audubon made his optimistic statement; the very last known pair was slaughtered, and its eggs smashed, in Iceland in 1844. So the great auk was probably the first North American species to be rendered extinct by the heavy hand of man; today only a few skins and eggs in museum collections provide evidence that this unusual and defenseless bird ever lived at all.

Early explorers and fishermen preyed one by one on all the sea birds of the northeast coast, but they did not find them all so prone to be slaughtered as the great auk. In fact, Cartier reported that gannets—as big as a goose, and with a formidable beak like the sharp end of a pickaxe—"bit like dogs." Rounding Newfoundland into the Gulf of St. Lawrence, Cartier came to Bird Rock, an immense hulk of stone rising more than three hundred feet from the sea. Shortly afterward an observer declared that "the birds sit there as thick as stones on a paved street"; and when Audubon visited Bird Rock in June of 1833 he found the nests so plentiful that they were "almost touching one another." At that time the number of gannets on Bird Rock was tremendous—perhaps a hundred thousand on its top and fifty thousand more along the ledges below. As Audubon approached, the island looked like "a white speck in the distance." Its top appeared as though covered with snow, and the air around it as though filled with snowflakes. Gannets are very large birds, with a wingspread of six feet. Their plumage is gleaming white, with a tinge of salmon-yellow on the back of the head, and black wing tips.

"I rubbed my eyes," Audubon wrote in his journal, "took up my glass, and saw that the strange dimness of the air was caused by innumerable birds, whose white bodies and black-tipped pinions produced a blended tint of light grey. When we advanced to within a half a mile, this magnificent veil of floating gannets, plainly seen, now shot upwards into the sky, then descended as if to join the feathered masses below, and again veered off to either side and swept over the surface of the ocean."

A whaleboat from the vessel Audubon had boarded managed to approach the island in spite of heavy surf, and to stay in its lee long enough for the men to kill some birds with clubs and guns. They also brought back a few eggs to the waiting naturalist, who observed:

The birds were seated on their nests, quite unconcerned. The discharge of the guns had no effect on those that were not touched by the shot, for the noise of the Gulls, Guillemots, etc. deadened the sound of the gun; but where the shot took effect, the birds scrambled and flew off in such multitudes, and in such confusion, that whilst some eight or ten were falling into the water either dead or wounded, others pushed off their eggs, and these fell into the sea by hundreds in all directions.

Audubon also reported on some rough and ready bird killing, or culling, in these parts which was characteristic of methods along the coast:

The whole surface is perfectly covered with nests, placed about two feet apart, in such regular order that you may look through the lines as you would look through those of a planted patch of sweet potatoes or cabbages. The fishermen who kill these birds, to get their flesh for codfish bait, ascend in parties of six or eight, armed with clubs; sometimes, indeed, the party comprises the crews of several vessels. As they reach the top, the birds, alarmed, rise with a noise like thunder, and fly off in such hurried, fearful confusion as to throw each other down, often falling on each other till there is a bank of them many feet high. The men strike them down and kill them until fatigued or satisfied. Five hundred and forty have been thus murdered in one hour by six men. The birds are skinned with little care, and the flesh cut off in chunks; it will keep fresh about a fortnight.

Later on, a lighthouse was built on this same rock, and passing fishermen who visited the top managed to reduce the birds to a fraction of their original numbers, before the Canadian government took action to protect the birds. Today the entire world population of gannets on both sides of the Atlantic comprises some 145,000 pairs, only twice the number Audubon saw on Bird Rock alone. Due to protection, their numbers have been increasing steadily from a low of 50,000 pairs in 1890.

It is still possible for a visitor to get some idea of the plenitude of birds seen by Audubon and the explorers before him at Bonaventure Island off the Gaspé Peninsula of Quebec. Like Bird Rock, Bonaventure Island was visited by bird hunters soon after its discovery by Cartier in 1534, as it probably had been by anonymous codfishermen before that. And until the Migratory Bird Convention of 1916 gave a measure of protection to sea birds, Bonaventure continued to be a regular stopping place for nest-robbers from ships fishing these waters.

Of the world's twenty-two gannet colonies, the six in North America are all in Quebec and Newfoundland. The one at Bonaventure is the largest such colony in the world. Creatures of habit, once gannets establish a breeding site they tend to return to it year after year. Knowledge of a colony in Britain goes back to the year 1274. Bird Rock and Bonaventure Island must have been occupied by gannets for a long time before Cartier came upon them in 1534.

Each April, the gannets arrive at Bonaventure in great white clouds, while snow is still on the ground, from wintering areas in the southern United States, Cuba, and Mexico. Each pair claims nine square feet of territory on a narrow ledge or the top of the cliff. To the eye as to the ear, the rock at nesting time is sheer pandemonium. There are endless territorial battles between the males, not only on the ground but in flight, and even in the water, where the birds may be seen trying to drown one another. To human ears the noise of the young birds begging for food, and the harsh cries with which the adults welcome mates back from hunting in the open sea, is deafening. It carries for long distances, and codfishermen declare that they use it as a guide when sailing in foggy weather.

The gannet does not use its sharp beak for spearing fish, as many people believe, but dives underneath its prey and then seizes it, beak open as it rises to the surface. The gannet's dive is headlong, straight as an arrow into water far beyond the surf, for most of its fishing is done in the open sea. If the prey is close to the surface, the gannet hovers over it at low altitude and then plunges into the water, but to fish in deep water it must dive from an altitude sometimes a hundred feet or more, so that the splash as it hits the water may gush upward as much as a dozen feet. The gannets can perform such dives without injury, due to special air-filled cells just under the skin which act as a spongy cushion against the impact with the water. These cells are part of a network connected with the larger air sacs and the lungs. Before a high dive the gannet inhales deeply, inflating the sacs and lungs with air.

Although the gannets are the most numerous and most spectac-

CORMORANTS

GANNETS

ular birds at Bonaventure, other kinds of sea birds nest there, too including the European and double-crested cormorants. Both can be seen farther down the Atlantic coast, especially during the winter, though the European species is less common. The two are similar not only in habits but in appearance—except at mating time, when the double-crested cormorant sports a ragged tuft of curled feathers on either side of its head. Although cormorants spend much of their time hunting fish at sea, their land origins are unmistakable. They may nest in trees as well as on rocky ledges, and they have some functional difficulty in fishing, since their oil glands do not work well and water gets into their outer feathers. After diving a few times, a cormorant becomes so waterlogged that it can barely fly. It flaps heavily to a nearby perch, spreads its wings and points its beak to the sky, holding this pose until the feathers have dried out. Nor are cormorants very good sailors, for instead of riding the waves like corks as do other sea birds, their heavy bodies sink until they are partly submerged, long necks pro truding with up-tilted bills above water. Nevertheless, cormorants do swim and dive for their prey with considerable speed and skill.

Cormorants have been depleted by man, in part because they compete with him for fish, even though the species they feed on are mostly of no commercial value. The feelings of many fishermen are summed up by Milton's description of Satan in *Paradise Lost*, sitting on the Tree of Life "like a cormorant." Indians, on the other hand, used these birds as food; their bones are the most abundant of all bird remains in the middens along the northeast coast. But cormorants were still present in vast numbers when European settlers arrived, and on the rocky islets where they roosted it was easy to club the birds to death at night. From about 1880 until 1920 there were no records of breeding cormorants in New England, but after only several decades of protection they have increased to such an extent that the U.S. Fish and Wildlife

Service has tried spraying their eggs with chemicals to keep them from hatching.

The offshore islands on which cormorants nest are usually treeless, though they were probably wooded to begin with. Wherever large amounts of the cormorants' guano falls, the trees eventually die. (Guano fertilizer, which is beneficial when cured, is obtained from the enormous island colonies off the coast of Peru, and the word itself derives from the Inca word *huanu* which means droppings.) After raw droppings have killed the trees, the birds build instead on rocky ledges, where they erect bulky nests of debris such as sticks, flotsam, kelp, and rockweed, nests which grow bigger with each nesting season.

A boat making an approach to Green Island off Witless Bay, Newfoundland, has to wait for favorable seas in order to land. It comes over waters black with murres and puffins crowded together like beds of mussels, where the puffins hop and lunge, feet behind them, floundering over the surface, rowing and breast-stroking with their short wings. To come upon these colonies is to enter another world, wreathed and shrouded, a region of tumultuous crying, white birds posted like sentinels on the rocky cliffs, the excrement from their nests streaking the rock like innumerable falls. The birds fly or tumble over the surface, and wheel overhead from all directions. Here is the excitement and stimulus, the mutual order, of great populations, and also their foreignness. The inhabitants stand at their own outposts in their own realm. Puffins, speaking among themselves in soft purrs and grunts, have the enigmatic charm of oriental dolls, with round white cheeks, indented eyes, spectacular triangular pinkish-orange bills, stumpy bodies, and vermilion legs and feet. They fly around the nesting cliffs like little heavy vehicles, sometimes with fish hanging out of their bills, and where they stand facing the sea, on bare or lichen-covered rock or the scanty turf, they perform short treading dances, almost pranc-

Common Puffins

ing on their toes. The murres ("turrs" in Newfoundland) call in a guttural or hoarsely melodic way; the cries of the graceful kittiwake are sharp and high.

Individual islands have different combinations of nesting birds. The densities of single species also vary from place to place. Gannets may predominate on one island, as at Bonaventure, murres on another. Each bird has its own kind of nesting site—cliff top, crevice, ledge, or burrow. Destructive competition is avoided by this ecological division of the breeding grounds. For example, Green Island has a breeding population of thick-billed and common murres, razor-billed auks, Leach's petrels, puffins, black guillemots, and kittiwakes, plus a number of herring and black-backed gulls. Along its cliffsides, the dark rocky ledges are crowded with gray-and-white kittiwakes and the curved black-and-white bodies, like so many carvings, of murres. They face outward, continually crying above swirling fogs and swelling seas. In Newfoundland, by the way, a country with some equally colorful place names, herring gulls are called blueys; saddle-back is the name for the great black-backed; tickle-ace for the kittiwake; tinker for the razor-billed auk; and hatchet-bill for the puffin.

The puffins, like petrels, make their burrows in the turf at the top of the cliff and along its slopes; or they may appropriate and enlarge a burrow made earlier by a petrel. After a while the ground is so honeycombed with burrows that they cave in and have to be dug out again. Kittiwakes construct nests out of seaweed and mud, making use of a very small space among the narrow niches and rocky steps on precarious heights above the shore. A few pairs of black guillemots, with sooty plumage, white wing patches, and vermilion feet, may be seen at a level near the water, nesting in crevices and between the boulders. Murres use open ledges for their nests, as do razor-bills, though the latter are inclined to choose a rather more sheltered location. Since all murres nest on bare rock with nothing but an occasional stone or pebble to keep their eggs from rolling off, it is surprising that their losses are not greater. It was once supposed that the pear-shape of a murre's egg prevented it from rolling; but the truth is that soon after they are laid, the eggs very often do roll, and since the nests are precariously situated they fall off ledges into crevices or shore rocks below in considerable numbers. But as Leslie M. Tuck explains in his monograph, *The Murres*, an egg that does not roll off in the first few days begins to be held more firmly in place by the gradual accumulation of sediment and excrement around it, and by the progressive change in the distribution of weight within the egg itself.

The egg on a rocky ledge, the murre's short and narrow wings for its deep underwater dives, a gannet's cushioned, shock-absorbent plumage are all adaptations to the marine environment. The seas that surround the tumultuous rookeries provide them their food, and are in turn so provided. The fish these birds consume—small cod, launces, capelin, or herring—are dependent on plankton, and the birds contribute to its production and to the whole marine economy by means of their excrement, which is washed off nesting islands by rain, spray, storms, and fog. Sea-bird excrement, rich in nitrates and phosphates, is basic to the growth of phytoplankton (floating plant life, as distinguished from floating animal life or zooplankton). After a heavy rain it clouds the waters around the nesting islands for miles.

The dense cold waters of the Northern Hemisphere sink under the surface during the winter, but rise upwelling in the spring at the same time that light favors the growth of plant life. The Labrador Current, which brings down pack ice in the spring, also carries masses of phytoplankton, diatoms by the million in every few square inches; the tiny animals of the zooplankton, whose reproduction is then encouraged, become unbelievably abundant. This seasonal "overturn" so favorable to life is assisted by the warm waters of the Gulf Stream carried into the north. Great stores of nutrient salts and minerals are brought up from the depths; the plankton flourishes; the fish school and feed by the millions over the shallow waters of the continental shelf; and sea birds crowd the islands.

Each species of sea bird has a chosen food and a particular zone for finding it. Kittiwakes and fulmars during the nonbreeding season travel on plankton, and the waste from merchant ships and trawlers. Black guillemots feed in shallow waters fairly close to shore. Murres hunt for fish, mollusks, and crustaceans in coastal waters, never ranging very far into the open sea but moving southward during the winter to Maine along with the common murres and to southern New England with their relatives, the thick-billed murres. The dovekie nests inside the Arctic Circle, but travels in winter over long ocean stretches down the coast, and feeds on minute creatures in the plankton, occupying both offshore and inshore zones. During the winter, puffins usually disperse individually or in small groups offshore, feeding on crustaceans and launces.

Except for areas out of the reach of protective laws and measures, conscious conservation is now the rule, and many sea birds are coming back in numbers. However, progress, even though it no longer slaughters wild birds for food or feathers, has indirect ways of persecuting them. Quite aside from possible long-term effects of contaminating sea water with atomic waste, and the destruction of food resources in the inshore environment by sewage and chemicals, by dredging, by filling and pesticides, sea-bird populations have already been drastically reduced by oil pollution. Although international agreements and legislation have alleviated the problem to some extent, they cannot prevent accidental cases. The wreck of the tanker *Pendelton* off Monomoy, Cape Cod, in January of 1951 was a disaster for sea birds, resulting in the destruction of 10,000 eiders, scoters, and oldsquaws. Crude and waste oil have a particularly disastrous effect on birds such as murres, razor-bills, and guillemots, which feed over coastal waters near shipping lanes. A small amount of oil can spread in a thin film on the sea for a long distance; a spot of oil no larger than a quarter on a bird's feathers can reduce their insulating properties so that it may die in cold weather. If a bird preens its feathers to rid them of the oil, it may get oil into its digestive system and die of poisoning.

The long arm of pollution can still reach the sea birds, even though their breeding sites are protected and relatively difficult to approach. Nevertheless, some birds, notably eider ducks, seem to have been increasing in recent years. Sea birds are still a tribe to themselves. One of the first sights to greet explorers from the Old World, they are still a living extension of the land they inhabit, allied with the sea and all its aspects—the huge, slow upheavals within its depths, the swells and storms of its surfaces, its fogs and ice and the wide air and open stretches that sweep the shores.

# THE HERRING GULLS

## 11

SEA-BIRD COMMUNITIES HAVE their own ancient, native habitats, their special marine feeding zones, and patterns of behavior that are fixed to some degree. With certain species, however, human agency has intervened to produce artificial conditions, and to cause the birds to change their habits and their ranges. The most obvious of these species is the herring gull, a bird so common along the entire North Atlantic coast that there is hardly anything, aside from salt water itself, more consistently in sight.

The herring gull breeds from the Arctic to as far south as New York in very great numbers. It winters from the Gulf of St. Lawrence and the Great Lakes to the Gulf of Mexico, numbering between 600,000 and 700,000, according to counts made in the coastal area alone. But it has not always occupied this sweeping range. A. C. Bent's *Life Histories of North American Gulls and Terns*, in 1921 named No-Man's-Land in Penobscot Bay, Maine, as the southernmost point of the herring gull's breeding range, though it also mentioned a small colony breeding near Martha's Vineyard. *Birds of Massachusetts*, by E. H. Forbush, published four years later, made the assumption that herring gulls had formerly bred on islands all along the coast of New England, but that human persecution had driven them away from the southern part of the coast. There was a time when their eggs were delicacies and their feathers much in demand by milliners. The protection of herring gull colonies gave them a chance to multiply again; but, as it turned out, laws may not have been essential. This bold, gregarious bird, scavenger and graceful flyer, has increased to such an extent that it is now considered a nuisance, even a menace, in some areas. Gulls in or near the cities may be a serious hazard to aircraft, flying across approach lanes or runways, or circling on updrafts high in the air. They are certainly a menace to related species of terns that breed in their locality.

Tern colonies on small islands are subject to all manner of interference, from rats, skunks, dogs, cats, and men. They are nervous and excitable birds that leave their nesting sites, sometimes permanently, on little provocation. Their eggs, laid in shallow depressions in the sand, are vulnerable to predators as well as to lengthy exposure to the sun. Herring gulls can knock out a breeding colony altogether, or help to do so in a material way. In the spring of 1964, about 250 pairs of herring gulls arrived at the traditional nesting sites of the common and roseate terns on Tern Island at Chatham, Massachusetts, and drove them away. The terns moved to nearby Monomoy Island and tried again, but their nesting was unsuccessful. (Successful nesting was reported in 1965.) It was a disastrous year for terns on Cape Cod, and similar losses of breeding areas in other parts of the coast seem to have reduced measurably their population. But the herring gulls, like human beings, to whom they are tied in many respects, continued to increase in population.

In less populous coastal areas of Canada and a good deal of New England, other kinds of gulls can be seen at intervals. Great black-backed gulls, which have also increased—though not nearly to the same extent as the herring gulls—stand on promontories, singly or in small parties. Kittiwakes, the only gulls to range beyond sight of land throughout the whole of the North Atlantic, crowd rocky cliffs during the nesting season. Bonaparte's gull, no larger than a tern and similar to it in flight, with white on the outer edges of its wings like the lining of a cloud, can be seen in winter along the coast from southern New England southward, and on inland lakes in Nova Scotia in the fall. Ring-billed gulls, suggesting a smaller version of a herring gull, are fairly common along tidal areas, often following in the wake of ships. The black-headed laughing gull breeds from Maine to the Caribbean and begins to appear in early spring along the North Atlantic coast, but during nonbreeding seasons its preference is for warm-water regions. Other members of the family, such as the glaucous and Iceland gulls, appear along southern coasts at intervals, and are something to watch for during the winter; but herring gulls are always with us.

In its natural state, assuming its relationship with human civilization to have some unnatural aspects, the herring gull has to fend for itself within the limits of what the coast provides for it and within the hazards of mortality, some of which this bird may add to by cannibalism. Watching the gulls away from cities along the coast, you can see that they avail themselves generally of the local food supply. They will eat all kinds of crabs, mollusks, and worms. They will eat dead fish in great numbers—as well as whatever live fish they can capture, though they are less expert than terns at diving from a height, being more inclined to settle or flop down into the water when snatching their prey. They will also eat adult and larval insects and the eggs and young of other sea birds as well as of their own species. But a strange new situation has now arisen. This bird, whose behavior is even shy in some parts of its range, has elsewhere become almost a parasite. In human terms, one would call it lazy and aggressive, dependent upon handouts. But it is well for those who cause a situation not to be too insulting to those who are obliged to act according to its results. The herring gulls are not responsible for open dumps, huge amounts of fresh garbage, pig farms, or the great traffic of modern fishing vessels up and down the coast. All this has made the difference between what was once a reasonably large population and one which is excessive.

Herring gulls can still be given credit for what they add to our shores. After all, they belong here, animals with the natural gift of soaring in all kinds of weather, of traveling many miles around the rims of the northern world, and inland to rivers and lakes far from the seacoast. We see them scattered into the wind, gray and white, somewhat flat-headed, with curved yellow bills and pale yellow eyes. Individuals among flocks ranged along the shore, on beaches or the water's surface, shifting forward from time to time as they rise into the air and beat their way up wind. Theirs is a windward-facing that belongs to this shore.

Their flying has long been admired and even imitated in the designs of human flight. Evolved for a life in the open spaces, gulls have light, long, and narrow wings that allow them to ride on currents of air. They sail close above the waves. They bank and plane down. They hover above a ship's wake, circling, or gliding with hardly a motion of their wings, using the wind deflected from the ship's hull. Sometimes they seem to swing with the wind over the sea, back and forth, with the play, the natural use and knowledge of it. They coast over the land against a strong spring wind, sliding to a side, circling back, moving forward again, alternately beating and soaring. Sometimes they tower thousands of feet in the air.

In the spring when freshwater herring, or alewives, begin to migrate from the sea, herring gulls gather sometimes by the thousands to mob them in shallow waters during the day. They carry off the fish, chase each other, letting the catch fall and then snatching it from each other in flight, and when they have eaten their fill they rest along the shore. When alewives come in during the evening, the gulls gather again against the pink and coppery light of the sun, swarming over the entrance to a creek or tidal estuary or standing in long rows along its banks.

During the winter months herring gulls flock in feeding grounds and roosts, but apparently as individuals rather than in pairs. They begin to pair up just before their arrival at their breeding areas in the spring, sometimes, so far as we can tell, recognizing each other immediately if they have mated during the previous year. New pairs mate after lengthy ritual and display. They nest on islands, as a rule, often making large nests on the ground out of grasses, sticks, seaweed, and other material. They lay three olive or grayish-brown eggs, spotted with black or dark brown, well concealed against the bare, rocky ground. The downy grayish-brown chicks grow feathers rapidly, and can fly in about six weeks. First-year birds are sometimes mistaken for a different species; they are dark brown with black eyes and bills. After the first spring molt their plumage is lighter; the bill is now flesh-colored with a black tip, and the eyes are paler. Full adult plumage is acquired in four years, or sometimes in three.

The great increase in the population of herring gulls is also attributable to their being opportunists, jacks of all trades, not just scavengers upon the bounty of human wastefulness. They miss no opportunity, but take advantage of whatever food they happen to find. In its first few weeks a chick has a fair chance of survival, provided it does not stray too far and fall prey to a marauding black-backed gull or an adult of its own species. In the critical stage before the young bird has become self-sufficient, it may still beg for food; but once it leaves the colony it must fend for itself.

The margin of safety at this point is a narrow one, and would ordinarily provide a natural check on the population; but that check ceases to operate when the young gulls are provided with a plentiful supply of waste fish and garbage. In exploiting their environment they are aided by remarkable eyesight. The topographic memory of gulls was demonstrated when three of them were deliberately removed from their range and carried to a place, presumably unknown to them, more than two hundred miles distant, during two successive years. In the second year of the experiment, the gulls returned to their nests in approximately a sixth of the time it took them the first year, probably because they had memorized landmarks and could take a more direct route back. The second important factor is that this same food supply can mean the difference between survival and starvation for young and adult herring gulls alike during hard winters, a limitation in any natural environment that has just so much food to go around.

Factory ships, trawlers, draggers down the entire length of the coast, working the waters of the continental shelf with an intensity that may eventually affect some fish populations, if it has not already done so, toss over great quantities of waste. The cleaning of fish is continual at fishery establishments on shore. During the summer, resort towns dump large amounts of refuse, as do metropolitan garbage collectors at all times of the year. In addition, gulls may feed at sewer outlets to the sea, at outlets of factories that dump food remains such as shellfish, and at gelatin dumps of commercial photography plants. Studies made recently under the direction of Dr. Drury considered the feeding problem in detail. They concentrated on six populations of herring gulls in southeastern New England, banding the legs of breeding adults and also coloring the birds themselves with dyes, a different color for each colony. Thus it was possible to obtain reports of sightings from the investigating staff and the public, showing the gulls' movements and distribution. For example, the green-dyed gulls from

HERRING
GULL

BLACK-BACKED
GULL

Cape Ann, near Gloucester, Massachusetts, were found to stay almost entirely in that area, although a few followed fishermen south to gather on Cape Cod. Red-tinted gulls from the Isles of Shoals, New Hampshire, were found as far north as Rockland, Maine, after the breeding season and, while a majority stayed near home, many drifted south as far as New York and New Jersey.

This study involved some complicated checking and correlation of the visits of breeding and nonbreeding populations to different areas, and of the distances they traveled at different times of the year. On the whole, the scientists found that gulls occupied a minimum range and used the food sources in it thoroughly. Large populations from one area did not all travel at once, or to the same feeding grounds. They divided their colonies into "suburbs," though each of these was within the radius of its colony's main, if scattered, source of supply. This had the effect of shortening the average commuting distance and lessening the overlap of feeding grounds—more efficient than if all gulls in one population had to fly the same distance to a plentiful but diffuse source of supply.

The studies also showed that breeding populations tend to remain distinct, with little overlapping. Some, for example those breeding at the Isles of Shoals, depend mostly on natural food, but those from the harbors at Salem and Boston feed heavily at dumps and fish piers. Others that breed south of Cape Cod range widely at sea and over offshore waters, feeding on natural food such as hermit crabs and scallops, refuse from draggers and other trawlers, as well as from inland dumps at Cape Cod. When adults are feeding the young, they concentrate on food sources closest to the colony. At this time a surplus of human refuse is important for the survival of the young, as it is also for young gulls that begin foraging for themselves in fall and winter.

Attempts by the U.S. Fish and Wildlife Service to reduce the population of herring gulls by spraying their eggs, so as to kill the embryos, were not successful and have been discontinued. All similar methods, such as poisoning and shooting, which do not deal directly with the biological cause of the gulls' increase, namely excess food, have had no real effect. New populations, with new food sources available at all times, replace the old. On the other hand, reducing urban pollution and modernizing fish handling processes can decrease the gull population simply by reducing the food supply. This has proved to be true at plants where roofs cover the fish while it is being processed, and where water used in washing fish is flushed directly into municipal sewers. At a dump south of Boston where there had been a population of between 4,000 and 6,000 gulls, the number dropped to a hundred within two weeks after a large incinerator had been put into operation. The number of gulls stayed down for nearly a year; but when trucks began dumping their loads in the open some distance from the incinerator on weekends, a thousand soon returned.

Herring gulls are equipped to take advantage of a situation which men have made. Other birds are not. Water birds, such as herons, that depend on food from marshes and tidal creeks, have declined greatly in numbers in recent years. Members of the night heron family are particularly vulnerable because of their preference for salt and freshwater marshes and the banks of tidal creeks and estuaries. When these are filled, sprayed, or polluted, the food of the herons may be drastically reduced. Insecticides lodged in the bodies of tadpoles, minnows, and crabs may poison the birds that eat them, as well as reduce the numbers of the aquatic animals themselves. Heronries, often established quite close to roads or houses, are likely to be violently disturbed or destroyed.

Along the shores of New Brunswick and Nova Scotia, gulls for the most part fly singly, standing about in occasional flocks, stalking in coves or looking for food on tidal flats. Traveling south on the Maine Turnpike, not until one reaches South Portland are they to be seen in big circling flocks, as they compete with pigs on a farm for garbage and mash. From there south they are all along the coast, still holding to their inherited disciplines, flying to roosts at sunset and leaving them again at daylight, gathering at dumps when the trucks begin arriving in the morning, moving on to the fish-processing plants, the tidal flats and shallow waters, or following after fishing boats—using whatever they can find, unwittingly increasing their race because of the wasteful habits of our own. They gather on our roofs, and follow us, calling raucously or harmoniously, personifications of the gray-and-white shore and symptoms, too, of our own strange ways of fitting to it.

# THE SHORE IN HUMAN HANDS

## 12

IT MUST SEEM to many urban or suburban dwellers that the North
Atlantic coast is what civilization makes it. But no matter how the
drama of human living may now overshadow the natural landscape, it was the other way around not very long ago. It might be
supposed that the natural environment on the fringe of megalop-

olis would have to be rediscovered by chance, recreated, and even imagined again; though the sea beyond us rocks and glitters as it always did.

Nothing we do can destroy nature and our ultimate connection with it. We merely hide and starve the environment, though we may be reaching the point where we recognize this as starving ourselves. Much of what we see is a shadow of the former reality: the alewife, shad, or salmon reduced to small numbers; the pied-billed grebe or the bittern, few and far between. It is an exceptional thing nowadays to see a bald eagle in the air. But in Maine or Canada you might catch sight of one with the recognizable white head and tail of an adult, on broad, brown wings floating high above the coastline. It turns freely and slowly under the sun, gliding with no wingbeat in the blue sphere of the sky, over green mountains or silvery waters, tilting very slightly. It rocks and soars and continues to glide on surely until it is lost to sight . . . a kind of guideline back to an invisible abundance, when ospreys and bald eagles used to fish and scavenge along all our shores, almost as thick as grackles are today.

The image of an unknown continental shore is gone with the stir and challenge it provided: the forests with their extreme risks and foreboding silences, the multitudinous fish, the unnamed birds, the plunging surf below cliffs shrouded in mist. What followed that image is nearly gone, too, the physical experience of making a living from the land and all the hard-earned knowledge that went with it. Ways of building a boat, of using seaweed for fertilizer and insulation, of taking fish in season, of knowing a shore—its fogs, currents, winds, temperatures, and tides—and of naming plants, even the simple practice of raising vegetables, are not easily replaced by education from a distance. To be told that milk comes from cows, or that carrots materialize from the living earth, is not the same as seeing it for yourself. Living on the land, of course, did not necessarily imply conservation. The history of the sea birds, the great depletion of shore birds at the hands of market gunners, the violent depredations on our land by farming before the advent of technology, the haphazard plundering of resources, the slashing and burning, and then moving on, prove otherwise. Yet alongside yesterday's rather poor land stewardship, the action of today's bulldozer in stripping an area of all its topsoil, grass, and trees in a few hours is the employment of mechanical oblivion.

There is hardly a square foot of land along the North Atlantic coast, or for that matter in America, where the effects of technology, sometimes controlled, but often close to vandalism, cannot be observed. Even the relatively open areas, not blotted out by "urban sprawl" have something in them to remind a man of the realities of his world. He might be crossing a highway, for example, heading for an untouched area of salt marsh with a beach on its ocean borders. He is reminded there of some town problems a few miles down the road, involving the complete erasure of an attractive area of freshwater marsh with an inlet touching it from the sea, with willows, alders, cattails. It was the kind of place someone with a sense of ease and proportion might settle, and in fact the white New England houses nearby proved that such was the case. A desert now supplants it, made of tons of sandy fill gouged out of a local hillside, which also had its natural attractions at one time. The fact that the developer was allowed to wreak this devastation upon the character of the town is the result of one unfaced and unstated problem—that the state laws protecting land were not as strong or as enforceable as the laws that protected the making of money.

He walks on, observing that a sterile accumulation of sand from years of highway maintenance has begun to choke an increasing amount of vegetation where the marsh borders the road. As he leaves the road, quickening his step to avoid the line of speeding cars spewing fumes behind them, he is reminded of something he has read—that vegetables and fruit raised near heavily traveled highways contain fifty per cent more lead than is considered safe for human consumption.

The waters of the inlet that bisects the marsh are spotted with gas and grease and moving scraps of waste paper, and its bottom is half paved with discarded bottles and tin cans. But the marsh as a whole is untouched; the sea air is cool and clean, though now our walker comes upon the body of a marsh hawk which appears to have been shot. There are few enough of those around. This year the ospreys that once nested alongside a series of ponds farther inland are not to be seen at all. By all accounts, the handsome North American population of this species is doomed. The contamination of its environment, and consequently its food, by pesticides, has led to sterility in the adults, unhatched eggs, and malformed young. The same thing seems to have happened to the local population of black-crowned night herons or "quawks," which once were abundant in the marsh area, roosting in woods above it and flying out to feed in its creeks and at the sea's edge.

Farther on, the walker finds the remains of a gannet, a winter casualty, its feathers stained by jettisoned oil from a ship. How easy it is to accept these things—a dead bird, oil on the waters, gas in the air—unless they injure you directly. Even so, who is to prove it?

Still, this marsh has been only slightly tainted in comparison with many other regions, and there beyond the limits of the shining salt-marsh grasses are the clean sands beside the sea. He saunters down to the beach and sprawls in the sand—to find himself tarred all over. The latest high tide has left a long line, far down the beach, made up of black gobs of waste oil. The smears on a man's skin and clothes can be washed away with a little effort, but for a bird they are ineradicable. So it is that both men and natural life take their chances on a world for which only the human species is responsible.

All natural environments, whether tampered with or not, are latent with nature's power of renewal, and every open stretch of marsh, field, and forest harbors elastic possibilities of growth. The web of life, as it has been called, stretches to encompass an indefinite number of specific communities, either potential or in being— ways and combinations in which organic lives can flourish. They live by each other's substance, and join in action. The swallow dips and swings down a tidewater ditch after insects, taking some of its motion and beauty from the food it requires. In salt-marsh grasses, above the line of high tide or where they can readily move away when the tide comes in, meadow mice have their innumerable runways in the surface of the peat. These mice are grass-eaters, though they will also take some of the many insects they find in the grass, possibly even the marsh snails that feed on decaying plant materials there. The mice are themselves the food of almost every preying mammal that visits the marsh—fox, weasel, mink, and skunk. Snakes feed on them, as do hawks, owls, and crows. The mice have a crowded and pitiable existence, and yet they constitute the power and sustenance of many lives other than their own. The distance that divides the lives of the swallow and the meadow mouse is filled with intricate designs for living and dying, all kinds of patterns involving mutual use.

Leaving aside for a moment the concrete, the asphalt, and the pollution, one begins to see the vast gap between the environment we produce and the one we have left behind. The North Atlantic coast is in a complex that ranges from the white, wind-driven wastes at the pole to warm, blue-green waves lapping sandy shores. It reaches southward from a region of tundra and stunted trees to a belt of spruce and birch that girdles the world, then to one of white pine, spruce, and the mixed hardwoods of the temperate zone. Throughout these thousands of miles, the gulls and guillemots, the hickory, oak, and elm, the sandworms and saltwater minnows, all take part in a synchronization, a tidal reach of lives. Each natural form represents a different set of opportunities in terms of the kind of natural environment it lives in.

What do we do with this universal depth and detail? We simplify it, or try to, using the quick methods, the over-all powerful methods, the convenient ones. We cover it up. We try to reduce its complexity and abolish some of its inconvenient energies, though nature, like a man suppressed, is likely to be brutal, giving back illness and poverty in exchange for confinement, letting loose an entirely new scourge for the one we think we have eliminated. Fill in a marsh, removing its great spongelike capacity that is a reservoir of moisture and a barrier against the sea, and you take your chances with shore erosion, with the runoff of rain water and the seeping of salt water into the supply of underground fresh water. The community that neglects its marshes, watersheds, and forest cover for the sake of quick and easy development may find eventually that its tax base has been eroded because it has destroyed its own physical foundations. Its houses will prove literally to have been built on sand because of the erosion of the complex soil cover, the reduction or pollution of its water supply, all its value gone along with the once clean air.

We have built a human world where the effects of our actions in one place are likely to be felt in another. The atmospheric belt that covers the earth like a film is no less subject to pollution than water is. Our technology discharges wastes into the air as well as into the lakes and streams. Once, the carbon dioxide released by our cities and our industry into the atmosphere would have been dissolved on contact with salt water; but by now, apparently, the discharge is too vast even for the ocean to absorb, and it does not dissolve. Other gases, radioactive particles, soot, and poisonous chemicals can be spread over great distances in this way. As the atmosphere spreads our wastes, so, of course, does the water. The river whose headwaters are polluted flows down to tidal flats and poisons the shellfish. It has been estimated that ninety per cent of all shellfish between Boston and Portland are contaminated. In Narragansett Bay, Rhode Island, federal officers have had to guard the shellfish beds at night against hijackers, for if this once pure and abundant but now polluted food were eaten, people might die of hepatitis. The Merrimack River, which rises in the White Mountains and has its outlet on the Massachusetts coast, has become so polluted, so choked with toxic pesticides, raw sewage, and chemical wastes that in some of its reaches it not only is poisoned but completely lacks oxygen. Since fish depend on dissolved oxygen in the water, the effect on their populations is disastrous. The effect on human beings may not be so direct and obvious as on a stray salmon or alewife; but in parts of this once broad and lovely river the sewage is so concentrated that mere spray against the front of a motorboat may subject its driver to serious bacterial infection.

If raw sewage and other wastes were treated by each of the communities through which such a river runs, the waters might recover some semblance of their former health; but so far it has been more convenient to use our rivers as open sewers than to respect their original nature. Industries on both the west and east coasts, especially those involved in making paper, have managed to devise new methods of treating fluid wastes so as to render them harmless. It has even been possible to restore a few salmon runs. But the engineering process involved is costly and complex, and in order to deal with the problem the same kind of action would have to be universal. Along much of the coastline, treatment of water supplies becomes increasingly more expensive and elaborate, but unless the process is maintained with all the ingenuity men can devise, there could well be mass fatalities. Many rivers running to the sea go there by way of the human alimentary canal. Cities are drinking human sewage, treated again and again.

A problem that will have to be faced increasingly in heavily populated areas along the shore is the encroachment of the sea, not just shoreline erosion but the penetration of sea water underneath the land. This has happened in parts of Long Island and might happen in the future on Cape Cod, both places having surface areas of glacial till overlying ancient beds of gravel, sand, and clay, with bedrock far below sea level. Buildings and paved highways have so covered the surface that rainwater runs off into streams instead of percolating downward through the soil. This cuts down on the underground supply of fresh water which ordinarily holds back the pressure of the sea. As a consequence, salt water invades the land, seeping in through the underlying sands and gravels.

These are only a few of the multiple effects of humans upon the earth they live on. Those actions touch things both great and small. In the region inundated by the human tide, much is either changed or destroyed. On Long Island, for all its remaining beauties, very few spring peepers are now left to sing in the months of March and April. To see a garden hoptoad is something of a rarity, though once it was so common as not to warrant a remark.

The exploitation will probably not end at the shore, but will continue seaward over the continental shelf, whose riches in minerals and food have not begun to be tapped. Perhaps we have margin enough to escape the consequences of our reckless haste, but it is more likely that we do not. Luckily, new attention is being paid to what remains of the natural environment and to what we are to do with it. Health, so far as man and nature are concerned, is a multilateral condition. We deplete the earth and we diminish ourselves.

We are in a new world of our own making, dynamic, changing, and in many respects devastating. It could hardly have been imagined two hundred years ago. In many areas the original vegetation has been so much cut over and replaced by other species— shade trees, cultivated crops, and weeds—that were never there before, that it is difficult to know what the native growth was. In numbers, wildlife always used to be ahead of us. Now very few natural lives escape our diminution of their habitats. They are having to compete with a new population which can take their resources away from them. Any given area of land supports wild-

Meadow Vole in Marsh Grass

life populations only up to a certain density. Land taken away by the squeeze of human numbers takes the wildlife with it.

Fish swim to the city's edge on a river tide and are left gasping away their lives on the bank because of the depletion of oxygen in the water. Factories run by atomic energy, requiring cold water for operation, may so raise water temperatures in an estuary as to have grave and damaging effects on fish and other natural populations. Time will tell, if we cannot. Ours is an experimental civilization, experimenting with its own "progress," experimenting dangerously with its mother earth. Man takes over a role formerly left to natural process, substituting his own works for the evolutionary products of a million years, and he marvels and shudders at his own presumption.

But nature still sets the limits to which men can go. Just as cliff-dwelling Indians of the Southwest had to abandon their homes after devastating years of drought, so western man can use up the entire underground water supply. He may survive by desalinating sea water, but so far no methods have been devised that are cheap and efficient. We are still in relative ignorance about our ability to farm the sea in the event that we begin to run out of food. Our risk-taking has its own inevitable dynamics and possibly its tragic outcome. Nothing ever guaranteed man's safety. Yet, concerning the natural universe, we are still curious, still inwardly aware of growth and seasons; our very sense of harmony is a part of nature. We crave room and the occasions of peace, and our cravings may yet contribute their effect to the kind of world we make.

Man's distortions of this balanced and multifarious environment, his reduction of its species, his fragmenting of its unities, are of such dimensions that he may seem to have reached the point of no return. He lacks the power to reverse his own actions. Yet the original stuff of the world is still intact.

# APPENDIX

## Natural Areas of the North Atlantic Coast

THIS LISTING of some fifty places to visit is not comprehensive. It has been prepared primarily for the visitor unfamiliar with the coast from Long Island to Labrador; it directs his attention to some of the highlights and particularly to places that offer a wide range of natural history attractions. Those who are fortunate enough to live along this coast will, of course, have their own favorite places.

### CONNECTICUT

*Hammonasset Beach State Park,* Clinton. A five-mile-long sand beach and extensive salt marshes make this an excellent place to see a wide variety of coastal birds. Best times to visit are spring and fall, since the park is overcrowded with visitors during the summer.

*Tern Sanctuary,* Old Lyme. Small colony of common terns on ledges. Nearby is *Great Island,* a large tidal marsh where many ospreys nest.

*George Treat Smith Game Preserve,* Milford: A small natural area, consisting of a thin strip of barrier beach with a salt marsh behind it, for shore plants and birds.

### MAINE

*Acadia National Park,* Bar Harbor. Concentrated view of the rocky shore, with jagged coasts, island-studded bays, cliff-bound coves. At Anemone Cave the sea has tunneled 82 feet into the rock and formed a cavern that glistens with sea anemones, coralline algae, rockweeds. At

Thunder Hole the incoming waves compress the air trapped in the cave and cause a resounding boom. Birds of Otter Head include sea ducks, guillemots, golden plovers. Somes Sound is a fjord running deep into the heart of Mount Desert Island. Do not miss renting a boat for a trip to Isle au Haut, a primitive five-mile-long island with untouched caves and cliffs. Some 50 species of mammals and 275 of birds have been seen within the park borders.

*Camden Hills State Park,* Camden. The third largest park in Maine, offering seacoast, marshes, and magnificent views of island-dotted Penobscot Bay.

*Lamoine State Park,* Ellsworth. Situated on beautiful Frenchman's Bay, the park affords an excellent view of Mount Desert Island.

*Machias Seal Island,* East Machias. Ten miles offshore, this treeless island has about 400 breeding pairs of puffins, 2,000 pairs of Arctic terns, 2,000 pairs of Leach's petrels.

*Monhegan Island.* Ten miles off the coast and reached by boat from Boothbay Harbor, Monhegan has the highest cliffs on the New England coast. The presence of the sea is best experienced during a storm when spray is sent over the top of White Head, a cliff about 100 feet high.

*Moosehorn National Wildlife Refuge,* Lubec. At the mouth of the Bay of Fundy, it is an excellent place to see shore phenomena: whirlpools, Fundy tides, thunderholes into which the tide pours with loud noise of compressed air, beaches with jasper-tinted sands. Although the refuge is devoted primarily to woodcock and ruffed grouse management, the visitor can also see many other birds and mammals, including harbor seals, moose, black bears, bald eagles, ruddy turnstones. At *Reversing Falls,* nearby, may be seen fresh water flowing down the rocks to the sea, tidal salt water coming upstream.

*Moosepoint State Park,* Searsport. Offers an excellent view of Penobscot Bay and the topography of a flooded river valley.

*Quoddy Head State Park,* Lubec. The park fronts on Passamaquoddy Bay and is across from Campobello Island where President Franklin Roosevelt had his summer home. Picturesque rocky cliffs rise sheer from the sea, and many shore and sea birds are seen.

*Reid State Park,* Woolwich. A small gem, one of the finest natural areas on the New England coast. In a compact area of less than 800 acres, the peninsula displays many aspects of the rocky coast: headlands, offshore islands, sand beaches and dunes, spruces growing down to the edge of the sea, abundant shore life.

*Scarboro Salt Marsh,* Scarboro. An extensive salt marsh with impressive numbers of typical water and shore birds.

*Todd Wildlife Sanctuary,* Hog Island. Many features of the rocky shore are seen here, including a fine spruce forest, various seaweed communities, birds.

## MASSACHUSETTS

*Ashumet Holly Reservation,* East Falmouth. Run by the Massachusetts Audubon Society, this reservation contains fine plantings of American holly, and wildflower walks are conducted in season.

*Cape Cod National Seashore,* administrative headquarters at Eastham. One of the largest expanses of undeveloped northeast shore is now preserved, keeping intact some 27,000 acres of beach, salt marsh, dunes, 150-foot-high cliffs, pygmy forests, kettle ponds formed by the melting ice of the glacier, the entire oceanside Great Beach.

*Castle Neck,* Ipswich. One of the finest dune areas on the whole coast lies between the tidal Essex and Ipswich rivers.

*The Lowell Holly Reservation,* Mashpee. A 130-acre reservation in Mashpee and Sandwich, containing unique stands of American holly. It is not advertised and somewhat hard to find; and perhaps in consequence, its woodlands and ground cover are unspoiled.

*Martha's Vineyard.* Five miles south of Wood's Hole, Cape Cod, this island is 20 miles long and 10 miles wide. There are multicolored cliffs and steep beaches along the north shore. On the whole, there is less for the naturalist than at nearby Nantucket and the Elizabeth Islands; but it offers more woods, ponds, and tidal inlets.

*Monomoy National Wildlife Refuge,* Chatham. Accessible only by boat, this is a ten-mile-long spit extending directly south from the elbow of Cape Cod. It is perhaps the last remaining area that can still be called wilderness on Cape Cod, since its use has been restricted by the U.S. Fish and Wildlife Service, which maintains it as a wildlife refuge. It contains fresh and salt water marshes, fresh ponds, and potholes, dense thickets, dunes, and sandy beaches. Great numbers of shore birds stop there in May and during the long fall migration from July to September. A nesting area for terns.

*Nantucket Island.* Once the whaling capital of the world, Nantucket seems to belong wholly to the sea, which washes about 80 miles of beach and is visible from nearly every part of the narrow, 14-mile length of the island. Practically no forests remain, but there are excellent shrub communities. Offshore is *Muskeget Island,* with about 20,000 breeding pairs of laughing gulls. *Tuckernuck,* another nearby island, is visited by an abundance of pelagic birds and waterfowl.

*Nauset Beach,* Eastham. One of the greatest concentrations of shorebirds on Cape Cod can be seen here. Nearby 10,000 birds congregate in the marsh behind the beach during the summer.

*Roland C. Nickerson State Park,* Brewster. This park, 1,775 acres in extent, has forest trees of considerable height for Cape Cod.

*Plum Island National Wildlife Refuge,* Newburyport. One of the finest shore areas in the state, with six miles of sandy beach, dunes up to 50 feet in height, a vast salt marsh. An excellent cross section of beach vegetation, ranging from beach grass to pitch pine, and a superb area in which to see shore birds and migrants.

*Salisbury Beach State Reservation,* Newburyport. More than three miles of sandy beach and shell mounds left by the Pentucket Indians are the main attractions.

*Sandy Neck,* Barnstable. Perhaps the best place on the northeastern shore for vegetation of a sandy beach, including sunken forests of pitch pine, areas of shrub and heather. The dunes are large and impressive, and there is an extensive salt marsh—both with representative plants.

*Stony Brook Valley,* Brewster. Here is a municipal beach, an undisturbed island surrounded by salt marshes, with a stream through which the alewives run up to inland ponds on their annual migration. Contiguous to the town property are 50 acres of marsh and woodland owned by the Cape Cod Museum of Natural History, which conducts weekly field trips in the area and to other points of interest on the Cape during the summer.

*Welfleet Bay Wildlife Sanctuary*, Welfleet. An excellent 650-acre preserve, run by the Massachusetts Audubon Society. Birding trips by beach buggy on Cape Cod shores, including Monomoy, are offered.

## New Brunswick

*The Bore*, Moncton. As the Bay of Fundy tide enters the estuary of the Petitcodiac River, topographical features cause the formation of a wave front that advances steadily upriver. This front is about three feet high, but at highest tides it may reach five feet. The tides, combined with frost, have sculptured *The Rocks*, an extraordinary formation at Hopewell Cape near by.

*Fundy National Park*, Alma. This very large park skirts the Bay of Fundy for about eight miles. Best views of the irregular shoreline and many coves are from the Herring Cove and Coppermine trails.

*Grand Manan Island.* Birds, spectacular red cliffs rising 400 feet from the sea, and fjords are the prime attractions of this island reached by ferry from Eastport, Maine. Large numbers of black guillemots nest in crevices in the cliffs. Nearby *Kent Island* has numbers of eiders, Leach's petrels, razor-billed auks, and the largest colony of herring gulls on the Atlantic Coast.

*Reversing Falls Rapids*, St. John. The reversing falls are produced by the rise of the Bay of Fundy tides and flow of water from the St. John River. At low tide, the river thunders through a rocky gorge and to the sea. But when the sea level rises as the tide comes in, the ocean water is higher than the river level; it forces the river water to reverse and flow upstream in a swirling mass of eddies.

## New York (Long Island)

*Bayard Cutting Arboretum*, Great River. In addition to unusual plantings, the arboretum has trails along the banks of a southern Long

Island tidal river There is a mature stand of swamp cypress, and many breeding shore birds may be seen.

*Fire Island National Seashore.* About 18 miles of undeveloped beach, salt marshes, and 30-foot dunes form a barrier island along the south shore of Long Island. The national seashore is of interest primarily to botanists on account of the unique Sunken Forest near Point O'Woods, with forests of red maple, blackgum, and other species, their trunks contorted by the wind, and their branches pruned back by the salt spray. On the protected bay side are excellent salt marshes, good growths of eelgrass, pure stands of reedgrass as tall as a man. Among the birds to be seen are nesting colonies of black skimmers, common terns, least terns, and black-crowned night herons.

*Hither Hills State Park,* Montauk. There is excellent dune vegetation, and the park is usually regarded as the best place on Long Island to see numerous kinds of unusual birds, including oceanic species.

*Jamaica Bay Refuge,* near Kennedy International Airport. Excellent year-round birding, one of the best places in the region for a variety of water birds, ducks, and geese in season, and the rare curlew sandpiper and ruff.

*Orient Beach State Park,* Greenport. A narrow peninsula of dunes juts into the Atlantic Ocean.

*Tobay Bird Sanctuary,* Oyster Bay. Virtually every species of shore bird known on the northeastern coast can be seen here at some time of the year.

## Newfoundland

The entire province, covering 40,000 square miles, is so undeveloped that almost anywhere outside of the towns and cities one will find wildlife in abundance, as well as rugged, deeply indented coasts. Some areas of particular interest are:

*Long Range Peninsula,* St. Anthony. This northernmost tip of Newfoundland is well worth a visit. It affords a good view of the Strait of Belle Isle and, across it, of Labrador; the Long Range Mountains, flat-topped, reddish granite cliffs, rise abruptly out of tundra vegetation.

*Terra Nova National Park,* Port Blandford. The newest Canadian national park, and one of the most outstanding, it owes its natural beauty solely to the sea. The coastline is extremely rugged, the result of the sea flooding a rolling landscape. Bold headlands point their prows out to sea, and fjords extend inland for great distances. Moose and black bears are plentiful, caribou can be found near the park boundaries, and there are numerous shore and sea birds.

*Witless Bay Islands.* Located 19 miles south of St. John's, these islands are among the finest places on the whole North Atlantic coast to watch sea birds, but they are difficult and dangerous to visit without a guide.

## NOVA SCOTIA

*Cape Breton Highlands National Park.* In the northernmost part of Nova Scotia, Cape Breton Island, this park cuts all the way across from the Atlantic Ocean to the Gulf of St. Lawrence, a total of 375 square miles of rugged land circled by the sea. The Cabot Trail, an auto road, winds around the park and offers interesting views of the geological structure. The most dramatic section is in the west, where hills rise sheer from the Gulf of St. Lawrence, and streams have cut deep gorges running to the sea. The diverse terrain provides habitats for many different communities of plants and animals, with fine spruce forests coming down to the sea, and abundant shore plants. Many kinds of birds can be seen, including Arctic terns, Bonaparte's gulls, sooty shearwaters, Leach's petrels, gannets, and other sea birds. Take the Middle Head Trail for an excellent view of the vegetation that grows on a headland stretching out to sea for about two miles; the effects of spray and sea winds can be seen in the contorted shapes of the plant species that manage to survive there.

*The Ovens,* Lunenburg. A series of deep caverns gouged out of the rocky cliffs by wave action.

## PRINCE EDWARD ISLAND

*Prince Edward Island National Park.* The park stretches along the north shore of the island, fronting on the Gulf of St. Lawrence, for a distance of about 25 miles between the towns of Cavendish and Stanhope. The broad sand beach is magnificent, with dunes and sandstone cliffs rising from it. The island was discovered in 1534 by Jacques Cartier, who described it as "low and flat and the fairest that may possibly be seen." This is still a good description. The shore is of interest because the coastline is irregular and presents a succession of deep bays and inlets between projecting headlands. There is a large nesting colony of great blue herons on Rustico Island.

## QUEBEC

*Bonaventure Island,* Percé. This island off the Gaspé Peninsula is noted for the largest breeding colony of gannets in the world, about 50,000 adult birds, and also for other colonial nesters such as kittiwakes, razorbilled auks, murres, black guillemots and a few Arctic puffins. Nearby Percé Rock is a 400-million-ton block of limestone, nearly 1,500 feet long and about 300 feet high.

## RHODE ISLAND

*Block Island.* Lying almost midway between Point Judith, Rhode Island, and Orient Point, Long Island, this island has a bold· rocky coast interspersed with dunes and beaches, and bluffs rising to 150 feet. Almost no trees remain, and the land down to the shore is covered primarily with grass and bayberry thickets. It is an excellent place for migrating and wintering birds.

*Goddard Park,* East Greenwich. A good sandy beach, dunes, and a marsh.

# SUGGESTED READINGS

### Exploration

BAKELESS, JOHN. *The Eyes of Discovery*. Philadelphia: Lippincott, 1950.

BREBNER, JOHN B. *The Explorers of North America, 1492–1806*. Cleveland: Meridian Books, 1964.

HOFFMAN, BERNARD G. *From Cabot to Cartier*. Toronto: University of Toronto Press, 1961.

HOWE, HENRY F. *Prologue to New England*. New York: Farrar & Rinehart, 1943.

OUTHWAITE, LEONARD. *The Atlantic*. New York: Coward–McCann, Inc., 1957.

WINSHIP, G. P. (ed.). *Narratives of Voyages Along the Northeast Coast, 1524–1624*. Boston: Houghton Mifflin, 1905.

### Specific Areas

BESTON, HENRY. *The Outermost House*. New York: Rinehart, 1949.

DUNCAN, ROGER F. and BLANCHARD, F. S. *A Cruising Guide to the New England Coast*. New York: Dodd, Mead, 1962.

HAY, JOHN. *The Great Beach*. New York: Doubleday, 1963.

KIERAN, JOHN. *Natural History of New York City*. Boston: Houghton Mifflin, 1959.

MORISON, SAMUEL ELIOT. *The Story of Mount Desert Island*. Boston: Atlantic–Little, Brown, 1960.

MURPHY, ROBERT CUSHMAN. *Fish-Shape Paumonok*. Philadelphia: American Philosophical Society, 1964.

RICH, LOUISE D. *The Coast of Maine*. New York: T. Y. Crowell, 1962.

THOREAU, HENRY DAVID. *Cape Cod*. 1865.

## Ecology

ALLEE, W. C. et al. *Principles of Animal Ecology*. Philadelphia: W. B. Saunders, 1949.

BERRILL, N. J. *The Living Tide*. New York: Dodd, Mead, 1951.

CARSON, RACHEL. *The Edge of the Sea*. Boston: Houghton Mifflin, 1955.

————. *The Sea Around Us*. New York: Oxford University Press, 1951.

CLARKE, GEORGE L. *Elements of Ecology*. New York: John Wiley & Sons, 1954.

KENDEIGH, CHARLES. *Animal Ecology*. Englewood, N.J.: Prentice-Hall, 1961.

MOORE, HILARY B. *Marine Ecology*. New York: John Wiley & Sons, 1958.

ODUM, EUGENE P. and ODUM, HOWARD T. *Fundamentals of Ecology*. Philadelphia: W. B. Saunders, 1959.

THOMSON, BETTY F. *The Changing Face of New England*. New York: Macmillan, 1958.

WILSON, D. P. *Life of the Shore and Shallow Sea*. London: Nicholson & Watson, 1951.

YONGE, C. M. *The Sea Shore*. London: Collins, 1949.

## Birds

DORST, JEAN. *The Migration of Birds*. Boston: Houghton Mifflin, 1962.

FISHER, JAMES and LOCKLEY, R. M. *Sea-Birds*. Boston: Houghton Mifflin, 1954.

GRIFFIN, DONALD. *Bird Migration*. Garden City: Natural History Press, 1964.

HILL, NORMAN P. *The Birds of Cape Cod, Massachusetts*. New York: William Morrow, 1965.

KORTRIGHT, FRANCIS H. *The Ducks, Geese and Swans of North America.* Washington: The American Wildlife Institute, 1943.

LOCKLEY, R. M. *Puffins.* Garden City: Doubleday Anchor, 1962.

PETERSON, ROGER T. *Field Guide to the Birds of Eastern North America.* Boston: Houghton Mifflin, 1947.

POUGH, RICHARD. *Audubon Water Bird Guide.* New York: Doubleday, 1951.

TINBERGEN, NIKO. *The Herring Gull's World.* London: Collins, 1953.

TUCK, LESLIE M. *The Murres.* Ottawa: Canadian Wildlife Service, 1961.

### Invertebrates, Shells

ABBOTT, R. T. *American Sea Shells.* New York: Van Nostrand, 1954.

BOUSFIELD, E. L. *Canadian Atlantic Seashells.* Toronto: National Museum of Canada, 1960.

BUCHSBAUM, RALPH and MILNE, LORUS J. *The Lower Animals: Living Invertebrates of the World.* Garden City: Doubleday, 1960.

MORRIS, PERCY A. *Field Guide to the Shells, Atlantic and Gulf Coasts.* Boston: Houghton Mifflin, 1951.

### Fishes

BIGELOW, HENRY B. and SCHROEDER, WILLIAM C. *Fishes of the Gulf of Maine.* Washington: U.S. Government Printing Office, 1953.

BREDER, CHARLES M., JR. *Marine Fishes of the Atlantic Coast.* New York: Putnam's, 1948.

HAY, JOHN. *The Run.* Garden City: Doubleday, 1959.

JONES, J. W. *The Salmon.* New York: Harper & Row, 1959.

NORMAN, J. R. *A History of Fishes.* (second edition revised by P. H. Greenwood). New York: Hill and Wang, 1963.

### Miscellaneous

BASCOM, WILLARD. *Waves and Beaches.* Garden City: Doubleday, 1964.

BERRILL, N. J. and BERRILL, JACQUELIN. *1001 Questions Asked About the Seashore.* New York: Grosset & Dunlap, 1957.

DEFANT, ALBERT. *Ebb and Flow.* Ann Arbor: University of Michigan Press, 1958.

HUBBELL, HARRIET WEED. *Treasures of the Shore: A Beachcomber's Botany.* Illus. by Marcia G. Norman. West Harwich, Mass: The Chatham Conservation Foundation, Inc., 1963.

MINER, R. W. *Field Book of Seashore Life.* New York: Putnam's, 1950.

MORRIS, PERCY A. *Nature Study at the Seashore.* New York: Ronald Press, 1962.

WHITE, LAURENCE B., JR. *Life in the Shifting Dunes.* Boston: The Museum of Science, 1960.

# INDEX